The Catholic Parents'
Survival
Guide

Other Books by Julianne include:

Braving the Thin Places: How to Create a Space for Grace in Your Life.

Start with Jesus: How Everyday Disciples Will Renew the Church.

The Catholic Parents'
Survival Guide

STRAIGHT ANSWERS TO YOUR KIDS' TOUGHEST QUESTIONS

Julianne Stanz

LOYOLA PRESS.
A JESUIT MINISTRY
Chicago

LOYOLA PRESS.
A JESUIT MINISTRY

www.loyolapress.com

Copyright © 2023 Julianne Stanz
All rights reserved.

Cover art credit: mrPliskin/iStockphoto/Getty Images, Tolga TEZCAN/E+/Getty Images,
Loyola Press
Back cover author photo: Mary Baird at Three Otters Photography.

ISBN: 978-0-8294-5517-5
Library of Congress Control Number: 2022952102

Printed in the United States of America.
23 24 25 26 27 28 29 30 31 32 Versa 10 9 8 7 6 5 4 3 2 1

To my Grandmother Nanny, whose strength of faith was a living catechism for her children, grandchildren, and great-grandchildren.

For Wayne and our three children: Ian, Ava, and Sean.

To parents, grandparents, guardians, teachers, and catechists—you matter in the life of each child you inspire, guide, and accompany in faith.

To the parents whose stories and insights are shared in this book, thank you from the bottom of my heart for your generosity.

Contents

Introduction:
It All Comes Down to Earth

You can know a smart person by the answers they give.
But a wise person by the questions they ask.
—Anonymous

This book starts with a question. What's the closest planet to heaven?

Think about it. Now think about it some more. What's the closest planet to heaven? How would you answer?

Now answer as if you were speaking to your own child. Tough question, isn't it?

As a Catholic parent who speaks and writes about faith regularly and ministers in the Church, I must admit that this question stumped me. All the more because it came from my son.

"Mom, what's the closest planet to heaven?" my 6-year-old asked. I was taken aback and didn't have an immediate answer. As an Irish woman, I'm not often stuck for words! My mind fumbled around searching for a meaningful response, but the depth of his question took my breath away. So, I told my son that I didn't have an answer right at that moment. He seemed surprised, but I promised him that, because the question was such a good one, I would try to find the best answer that I could. "OK," he said, "but make sure to let me know, because I've been thinking about it a lot."

I thought about it a lot too.

The answer took me a few weeks to address and work out for myself. Without getting into too much detail, such as reminding my son that heaven is a state, not a specific location, I picked through various answers and opted for a simple one.

"The closest planet to heaven is Earth, son," I told him. "Jesus lived here and shows us the way to get there. The way to get to heaven is from right here," I said, gesturing around us. "Right here on Earth is where we were yesterday, where we are today, and where we will be tomorrow. The closest planet to heaven is Earth."

He seemed satisfied enough. But was I?

As a parent who has multiple advanced degrees in theology, I was shocked to realize that all my years of formal study did little to help me address the practicalities of my children's questions and, indeed, even how to frame my answers for their understanding. Until I became a mother, I did not realize how deficient my studies would be from the practical perspective of answering my children's questions. I received an excellent education, but it did not equip me to address the faith questions of my children in a way that was simple, clear, coherent, and compelling. I often thought, *If I can't address these questions in a way that feels satisfying for my own children, even with my continued years of theological study and formation, something is wrong.* "How were you prepared to share your faith with our children?" I asked my husband. "I wasn't really," he said. "It's trial and error mostly." Does this feel familiar? It does to many of my friends who are parents and who have shared this sentiment with me as well.

I can certainly relate to feeling inadequate in the face of the seemingly unrelenting questions of my children! "Why, why, why?" seems to be the mantra of young children in elementary school. But as they get older, our children in high school and college often stop asking questions about faith. Is it because they are no longer interested? Or

"My parents just don't know how to answer my questions so I stopped asking."

In sharing this experience with other parents, I also realized that knowing how to answer questions about faith is not enough. What also matters is how we address these questions through our body language, tone of voice, disposition, and willingness to listen and engage. Sharing accurate and precise information isn't enough. Information must be balanced by our own openness to dialogue and to meeting our children "where they are." Conversations about faith must also be reinforced in the culture of a home that puts faith at the center of faith life rather than marginalizing it in favor of extracurricular activities and the endless rushing of the world. Yes, formation and study are important, but the context in which we live our faith in the home is more important than any class about religion. When it comes to conversations about faith, things aren't cut and dried. Parenting is messy because life is messy.

And that's the point, right? Faith is not precise. *Faith is a lived relationship with Jesus Christ and the community that he founded, the Catholic Church.* Equipping our parents with some basic information to address their children's faith should be an important part of our efforts to reach our families so that our Catholics can remain Catholic. As a Church, we certainly talk about the issue enough!

"Keeping our children Catholic" is a continual talking point among all Catholics today, especially because the research is sobering and grim. Released in 2017, a survey titled *Going, Going, Gone: The Dynamics of Disaffiliation in Young Catholics* sought to describe more fully, and in young people's own words, why they had left or were considering leaving the Catholic Church. One of the statistics that perturbed many, and rightly so, is the stark reality that 74 percent of young people indicated that they stopped identifying as Catholic between ages 10 and 20, with a median age of 13.

Every time I share this statistic at conferences, talks, parent retreats, and so forth, there is an audible gasp from those in the room. Every. Single. Time. This statistic cuts deep and strikes a nerve. Even those who do not practice their own faith regularly seem to be rightly bothered by this. The fact is that it *should* unsettle and bother all of us. As the popular expression goes, "The struggle is real, folks!" At the heart of this issue lies the reality of parents just like you and me grappling with how to talk to our children about faith, how to share our faith as a family, and how to keep our children Catholic. This struggle affects our families, and it affects society. In a world where young people suffer from increased rates of depression, anxiety, and suicide, young people long for meaning, authenticity, and community, just like the rest of us.

Many parents and grandparents regularly comment to me that books typically marketed to Catholic families are often very homogeneous in their approach and outlook. Many Catholic writers often presume that the Catholic family of today is a "typical" two-parent family where one parent stays home with the children, there is support from a strong extended family, and grandparents and relatives are present. Such books are often written with little regard for any kind of diversity within the family context and the wider world, and they are written from a very catechetical or educational perspective, aiming for clear teaching but with scant regard for the context in which we live today. Many parents have shared with me that they long for a book that recognizes the reality of Catholic families today and the difficulties of raising children in a world that does not always seem very receptive to faith.

Modern Catholic families are composed of people who are at all different stages of growth in faith, at all different stages and walks of life. There are blended families, families with no extended family or none close by, single-parent homes, and homes with "boomerang children" in which college-aged adults live at home because the cost of college or owning a home is so expensive. All of these are Catholic families.

Many parents have told me that they dread their children's questions, particularly questions about faith, for the following reasons:

- They are afraid that a questioning child leads to a doubting child. (It doesn't!)
- They are afraid that they won't know how to address their children's questions correctly or compellingly.
- They are afraid that their children will see the disconnect between what they (the parents) say they believe and how they act.

A Book Designed to Assist Parents in Conversation with Their Children

This book draws on a vast array of experiences from real-life Catholic parents and includes simple, practical, and "parent-tested" ways to share your faith. Great tips and ideas will be offered but so too will mistakes and failures.

This is not a grand book that makes sweeping promises such as "If you read this book, you can keep your children Catholic." I know better than that, and so do you. This book is designed to be simple, direct, and helpful—it's meant to assist you as a parent to address your children's honest-to-goodness real questions and to share age-appropriate and Christ-centered information with your children today. Children hear a lot of "what the church teaches" in their faith formation classes or in Catholic schools, but we don't often address the *why* behind the *what*. This book lays a foundation for the *who* and the *why* (Jesus) before the *what* and the *how* of the church's teachings to help you to make the connection between faith learning and faith living in the home. I share questions from real children across the country and how parents actually responded to these questions. I also share questions from parents and answers from other parents. You might choose to respond differently than the answers given here, but at least you will have an opportunity to learn from the wisdom of others, and that includes the church's teachings on many topics, including morality.

This book features real parents and grandparents addressing children's toughest questions and draws on a wide variety of parental perspectives with the following goals:

- To guide you to take incremental steps to grow your own faith and the faith of your children
- To equip you to address tough questions
- To help you provoke curiosity about Jesus and his teachings
- To understand how the church of the home and the parish church are connected
- To help young people formulate their own responses to difficult questions

The end of each chapter features the section "Take It Home," which includes a summary, prayers, resources, and some helpful strategies to continue living out the key concepts outlined in the chapter.

"The closest planet to heaven is Earth," I reminded my son as we discussed his tough question, and so it's fitting that this book model a very down-to-earth approach. Earth is, after all, our home, and what we do here determines what happens in our next life: our eternal home.

In the pages to come I refer to parents and grandparents, but if you are a teacher or a catechist, this book is also for you. We can all tap into the wisdom of the lessons shared throughout the book.

So, let's start on our journey with a tour of some back-to-basics teachings and questions you are likely to encounter about the *who* behind the *what*: God, Jesus, and the Holy Spirit. Speaking of the Holy Spirit, this book may feel like a whirlwind at times, so hang on to your hat and enjoy the ride!

1

Parents as Arch-Influencers

It might seem a bit of an odd way to begin a book about answering your children's questions by starting with adults. But trust me, there's good reason for this. I want to take you to one of the most interesting places in Ireland to emphasize a simple but profound point about the need to start with our own faith as adults before we discuss the faith of our young people.

Jesus, Mary, Joseph, and the Cup of Tea

One of my favorite stained-glass windows is in County Galway, Ireland. At the rather long-named Cathedral of Our Lady Assumed into Heaven and St. Nicholas, the window has become a place of pilgrimage for many because of its unusual depiction of the holy family. Called "The Window of the Holy Family," it beautifully depicts Jesus, Joseph, and Mary in a very ordinary yet accessible manner. In the background, Joseph, his sleeves rolled up, works on a carpentry project. In the foreground, a young Jesus with red hair (this is Ireland, after all!) brings his mother, the Blessed Mother, a cup of tea! Every time I bring a group to see it, they smile or laugh to see something as ordinary as sharing a cup of tea elevated to the heights of holiness. As for the Blessed Mother, she is seated and knits an item of clothing, barefoot and clad in a simple blue robe. The glasswork is exquisite, the colors rich and vibrant. This window continues to captivate people after generations because it emphasizes a beautiful point of our Catholic faith: of all the ways that God could have made himself known to his people, he chose the family to reveal his great love for us.

Jesus was born to a humble family in the raw poverty of a stable. It was in the family that he learned the most important practices of faith—where he learned how to pray. It was within the context of the family that he was presented at the temple. It was the family that provided Jesus with the security and safety from which to launch his public ministry. It was in the family that humanity experienced God's love for the first time.

This point cannot be overstated: *it is in the family that we first learn who God is, what we believe about our faith, and why our faith is important.* It is in the home where our children learn how to know, love, and honor God and to grow in holiness. A family is holy not because it is perfect but because God is already present in each of our families. This is why the Catholic Church refers to the family as "the domestic church." There is no greater building block of faith than the family, and it is important to remember this, because many parents, grandparents, and guardians mistakenly believe that they have little influence on the faith of their children. Let me share with you a little story to illustrate this.

Ava and the Bishop

The entire body of Catholic bishops in the United States typically meets twice a year for their general assembly, where they address matters pertaining to canonical and civil matters. Attendance is limited to the member bishops and to individuals and organizations who work in conjunction with the United States Catholic Conference of Bishops, or the USCCB. I have served as a consultant to various committees at the USCCB for many years, and so my children have gotten used to what they call "Mammy's work with the bishops."

A few years ago, my family came with me to the November general assembly. After the last meeting had ended, my husband and I agreed to meet in the lobby of the hotel so that our family could go to dinner. On the elevator down to the lobby, I was talking with a particular bishop I know well and have worked with for many years. We stepped out of the elevator together, and my daughter ran up and gave me a hug. She was 5 years old at the time and quite the chatty Cathy, as the expression goes!

"My name is Ava!" she proclaimed. Then she asked the bishop with much eagerness, "Do you know Jesus?"

"Why, yes, I do!" he exclaimed with delight. "I often spend time talking to Jesus in church."

"That's so cool," my daughter said. "We do the same in our house, and sometimes I even talk to him at night before I go to sleep."

"That's really great, Ava," he said. "It's so important to talk to Jesus every day."

"So, what do you do?" she asked him while twirling around the lobby of the hotel.

"I'm a bishop," he explained to her, "and part of my job is to make sure that the faith that Jesus handed on through the apostles is kept safe so that we can all talk to Jesus anywhere that we need to."

During this exchange, the bishop had bent down a bit to talk to Ava at eye level. But after this last statement, she stepped back, looked right up at me and asked, "Is that true, Mom?"

The bishop chuckled (thanks be to God!), and I said to Ava, "Yes it is, and your father and I will tell you all about the bishops and their roles, a little bit later." For the time being, she seemed satisfied enough.

As I was turning to say goodbye to my bishop friend, he remarked: "It's true the world over, Julianne. Children will not believe the word of a stranger when it comes to faith in Christ, but they will look to their mother and father first before anyone else, just as Ava did today. We should never be afraid of the questions that our children ask." He waved goodbye to our family.

This exchange reveals an important truth: when it comes to matters of faith, children will often verify what they hear and see through the relationships that are closest to them. Ava was not willing to believe the word of this particular bishop, but she was willing to believe the word of her parents. In fact, she looked to me to verify the truth of what the bishop had just told her. The word *verify* comes from the early fourteenth-century Old French *verifier* and from Medieval Latin's *verificare*, which means to "substantiate or to find out the truth about." As parents, we often verify for our children what is true and what is not, especially in matters of faith. Therefore, parents exert a huge influence on the faith of their children. We might consider parents influencers par excellence.

What, Me? An Influencer?

In the past decade, we have become familiar with the term *influencer*, which is used primarily to describe those on social media who build a reputation around certain topics or products. Influencers are often paid by companies (through cash or other incentives) to influence how other people make decisions. For example, beauty brands often pay attractive men or women (usually celebrities) to talk about certain products such as makeup or skin care lines on their personal social media pages. For young people often skeptical of authority, influencers are far more credible than the corporations that stand behind them.

However, when it comes to our children, research continues to bear out that the single greatest influence on children's faith is their parents or other significant adults in the role of parent or guardian or mentor. That might seem scary for us as parents, especially if we are unsure about certain aspects of our own faith, but it is true. Mistakenly, we often believe that we are just one factor among many, but Justin Bartkus and Christian Smith's *Report on American Catholic Religious Parenting*, published in 2017, indicates that parents are the most important factor in the faith development of their children. The authors remark on page 8 of this study that "parents represent not simply an influence on the development of children's religious world-views, but the arch-influence over it." As "arch-influencers," then, we cannot underestimate our importance in influencing our children's faith. You, the parent, matter. So does the presence of other adults in the lives of children: grandparents, aunts and uncles, close friends, other adults in the faith community, and godparents, for example. Each adult your child encounters can influence the development of their faith, whether we are conscious of it or not. As parents, we can become so caught up in the lives of our children that we forget about our own faith and making sure that it is as strong as it can be.

Children, youth, and young adults want well-reasoned answers to their faith questions, and in an age when they can Google many of these questions on the internet, the question-and-answer dialogue is even more important, so that they can receive sound, accurate, and balanced information. If we want our children to have faith, then we must have faith ourselves. If we want to be able to answer our children's questions, then we need to grow in our understanding of the Catholic faith no matter how much or how little education in faith we have received. We cannot lead our children to Jesus until we have gone to him ourselves.

Faith as Oxygen

When flight attendants provide instructions before takeoff, they remind us that if the airplane goes into a state of distress, we should always secure our own masks first before helping anyone else, and that includes our children. There's a good reason for this. If you helped someone before yourself, you could run out of oxygen and pass out, and then you would be of no good to anybody.

This analogy holds true when it comes to the faith of our children. If we want our children to breathe into their faith, then we must make sure that our own oxygen supply is strong first. Putting on the oxygen mask of our faith is as simple as committing to continually learning and growing in our understanding of faith, cultivating a regular prayer life, going to Mass, receiving the sacraments regularly, and sharing our faith with others in word and deed. OK, we all know that it is far easier to talk about faith rather than live it out, but that's why keeping our own oxygen flowing is so important for our children. The health of our family is dependent on our own health as the two ebb and flow together. In addition, as we strengthen our own faith, we will be able to more fully withstand the barrage of questions that surely comes our way! So, let's talk a little about the value of questions and answers.

Out of the Question

> *Be patient toward all that is unsolved in your heart and try*
> *to love the questions themselves. . . . Live the questions now.*
> —Rainer Maria Rilke

A study conducted by Michael Chouinard titled "Children's Questions: A Mechanism for Cognitive Development" found that children between the ages of 3 and 5 ask as many as seventy-six questions per hour! The basics of questioning—who, what, where, when, why, and how—guide us in navigating the world around us. While we retain our inquisitiveness and curiosity about the world as we age, the frequency of questioning declines with time.

Jean Piaget, the noted Swiss psychologist and genetic epistemologist, is most famously known for his theory of cognitive development that explored how children develop intellectually. Piaget's research indicates that children pass through four stages of intelligence and formal thought processes.

1. The *sensorimotor* stage, which lasts from birth to approximately age 2. In this age, children primarily come to know the world through their senses and motor movements.

2. The *preoperational* stage, which lasts from age 2 to age 7. It is characterized by the development of language and the emergence of symbolic play.

3. The *concrete operational* stage, which lasts from age 7 to approximately age 11, during which logical thought is emerging, although children still struggle with abstract reasoning and thought.

4. The *formal operational* stage, which lasts from approximately age 12 into adulthood and is marked by more abstract thought and deductive reasoning.

Younger children more frequently ask questions of the who, what, and how variety, such as, "Who is God?" "What is faith?" and "How are babies born?"

Older children, however, increasingly ask more existential questions, such as, "What is my purpose in life?" "Why are we here?" and "What difference does faith make to my life?"

Young people and young adults today have grown up during a time when the internet makes searching for the answers to questions much easier. With this ease of information, however, comes a proliferation of different opinions, and that makes curating accurate information, particularly when it comes to faith, even more critical. As a result of the ease with which we can search for questions, there is an important shift to be aware of when it comes to the types of questions to listen for as a parent. Young people can more easily search online than ever before to find answers to the simple what and how questions of faith, *but they can learn about a lived faith only in relationship to others.* The deeper, more existential questions cannot be satisfactorily answered online; it takes *you* to mediate these kinds of questions.

If you are not sure how to answer the questions your children have, whether simple or more complex, you are not alone! In the coming chapters, we will delve into all kinds of interesting questions. But before we do so, I want to introduce you to a helpful technique to address questions; it's called the Socratic method. Developed by the Greek philosopher Socrates, the Socratic method invites you to ask children what they believe about a particular issue by posing the same question back to them. Take the following question for an example: "Daddy, why do we kneel at Mass?" This is a relatively simple question. But rather than supplying the answer, the Socratic method urges you to pose the same question back to the child. "That's a great question, Maddie—why do you think we kneel at Mass?" This allows you as a parent to understand the underlying motivation for the question, any preformed ideas your child may have gleaned, and the opportunity to open up dialogue. The exchange of questions helps the child feel listened to, respected, and heard.

But don't just take Socrates's word for it! This method was effectively employed by Jesus, who was asked all kinds of questions in the Gospel accounts of his life. Here are some examples of questions Jesus used and posed back to his followers.

- What do you want me to do for you?
- Who do you say that I am?

- Where is everyone?
- What are you looking for?
- How much do you love me?

Sometimes it is appropriate to answer a question clearly and simply. Too much information too soon can douse the fire of curiosity. Let the child lead the way, and then trust your instinct. Pose interesting questions to your children and listen attentively to them as they voice their hopes, fears, and dreams. As a friend of mine is fond of saying, "Do not drown a teaspoon of a question with a gallon of information." Turning a fire hose of information on people is not effective. Brains need time to process, and after a while people switch off. Questions are the building blocks of a life of faith, which leads me to a point about being intentional in how we speak about "faith" with our children.

"The Faith" Is "Your Faith"

Once after I gave a talk to a group of parents about simple but important ways they could help their children grow in faith, a man named David approached me. "I have five children at the moment ranging in age from 8 months to 10 years," he said. He then asked a very important question: "What's the best way to pass on the faith to children?" Read David's question once again. Now, does anything strike you about the question? Any turn of phrase that seems unusual? When I was reflecting upon this conversation later, it struck me that many of us ask the same question using the exact same words: "How do I pass on *the faith* to my children?" The key lies in the phrase "the faith." How many times have you heard people talk about "the faith"? How often have you used the phrase "the faith" to describe your own faith life?

Many times we talk about faith as if it were a product or a commodity. We speak of faith as if we were passing along a manual of instructions rather than a living relationship with God. "Hey, son (or daughter)! Read this and you will have the faith" seems to be the implication for our young people. The expression "the faith" often implies an impersonal product that we can pass along rather than a living, breathing, and changing relational dynamic. For Catholics, study and education about our faith are tremendously important, but ultimately faith is a lived relationship with God, and it's a way of life. Faith means nurturing a personal relationship with Christ, who is the same "yesterday and today and forever" (Heb. 13:8), and living out that relationship through our Catholic faith. It is important to remember that we are sharing not just the message of Christ but also his very person. Jesus is the Good News, and while faith can certainly be "taught," it is more often "caught," as the next little story underscores nicely.

Caught, Sought, and Taught

A few years ago, I went home to Ireland to visit my family and took my son and my two nephews out for a walk and some ice cream. My son Ian was a year old at the time, my nephew Sean was 3 years old, and the oldest nephew, Michael, was 4. They were a handful! After we had eaten our treats, we clustered in the cafeteria for a few moments as a summer rain shower passed overhead. I remember vividly that the day was a hot one, and little rivulets of steam and water collected on the lane outside the café. After the rain stopped, the three boys ran outside to splash and play in the muddy puddles (their mothers were not too pleased with the state of their shoes when we got home!). Suddenly Sean took a pause from playing and bent down in the puddle of water. He scooped up some water and put his hands to his head and smiled. It was the expression on Sean's face that made me reach for my camera, for his face was quite solemn, reverent, and a little intense. Michael began to do the same thing, and then my little Ian, who could not walk at the time, scooted to the edge of the puddle to put his hands in the water. *What were they doing?* I wondered as I snapped some quick pictures.

That evening I asked Sean's mother about the incident, and her face lit up with joy as she explained what was happening. Sean and his grandmother would often stop on their weekly shopping trips for a few moments in church to pray and reflect. Each time they entered and left the church, Sean's grandmother would encourage him to bless himself with the holy water. This practice became ingrained in his little 3-year-old heart and mind, a practice that his grandmother had taught him. Every time we enter and leave sacred space, we make the sign of the cross and bless ourselves.

Somehow, in this ordinary puddle of rain, Sean was reminded of the extraordinary abundance of God's love and our ability to give witness to it. Michael, seeing Sean bless himself, was moved to do the same himself. He "caught" what Sean had been taught by his grandmother: a sense of the sacred in the ordinary, a reminder of God in a shower of rain. My little Ian, who could not yet coordinate the blessing of his body, touched the edge of the puddle to share in the moment also.

This image remains an image for me of "faith taught, caught, and ultimately sought."

- *Taught:* faith is a relationship where knowledge and study enhance and strengthen it.
- *Caught:* faith involves witness, practice, and tradition.
- *Sought:* faith, even when not well understood, still can have the capacity to profoundly touch our lives.

As a parent, I have come to realize how important it is to be a visible witness to Christ in the ordinary moments and puddles of life. We must deepen our own faith in order to believe in the Gospel message, to seek opportunities to grow in faith, and to go forth to boldly proclaim the Gospel with courage and joy. When this seems difficult, please remember the three little Irish boys—faith caught, taught, and sought—in a humble puddle of water. What we plant in our children's hearts, in time, and when we least expect it, will be showered by God's grace and bloom!

Our children will ask a lot of questions, but they will also watch, listen, look, and learn in all kinds of ways. The dialogue we have with them is important, but so too is the way we live the questions that our children ask! If the way you live and the questions that your children ask are in harmony with each other, your children will come to understand that faith is at the heart of your family in ways you won't even have to point out. Faith will be interwoven into everything you do as a family.

Remember that there are no "bad questions," because all dialogue is a bridge between faith learning and faith living. So, lean into these moments and enjoy the opportunity to intentionally talk with your children about your faith, especially when it comes to the basics, which are not basic at all. Now let's turn our attention to some of the basic building blocks of our faith.

Take It Home

Key Takeaways

- You are the most important influence on the faith of your child.
- Passing along your faith is a living dynamic because faith is relational.
- Putting on the oxygen mask of your own faith will keep faith flowing to your children.
- Remember the Socratic method.
- Exchanging questions is a way to grow in faith as a family.

Reflect and Journal

Think about the kinds of questions that your children usually ask.

Are they *what* questions? *How* questions? *Who* or *why* questions?

Which are the most difficult?

Would you consider your faith to be more taught, caught, or sought?

Who had the biggest influence on your faith?

Take some time to reflect upon your own faith.

Personal Faith Inventory

	Always	Often	Sometimes	Rarely
I have a personal relationship with Jesus, and am growing as a disciple.				
I actively try to model my faith to my family and friends.				
I go to Mass every Sunday.				
I read the Bible every day.				
I find time to pray each day.				
I spend time studying the teachings of the Catholic Church.				
I go to the Sacrament of Penance.				
I understand and try to practice the spiritual and corporal works of mercy.				
I know the importance of serving the poor and actively try to do so.				
I invoke the intercession of the Blessed Mother and the Saints.				

Pay attention to the areas that are growth opportunities for you.

- Which areas are the strongest?
- Which area would you like to improve?
- What is one tangible step that you can take to develop your faith?

Practice: The Socratic Method

Think about a hot-button topic your children have asked you about. Practice your response with a friend, a family member, or another adult by using the Socratic method. Was this approach helpful? What did it teach you?

Pray: For God's Help in Parenting

God our Father, author of life and from whom all blessings flow,
> I thank you for the gift of being a parent (grandparent,
> teacher, catechist).

My children are among my most precious gifts from you.

Guide me in leading my children to you.

Strengthen me in faith, especially in times when I am afraid,
> upset, and angry.

Remind me to call upon you when I forget you.

Be with me, Lord, in the highs and the lows,
> the peaks and the valleys.

Help me, Lord, to remember that I too am your beloved child.

I praise you for the gift of life.

In your most precious and holy name I pray,

Amen.

Take some time to reflect upon your own faith. On a scale of 1 to 10, with 1 being "weak" and 10 being "strong," how would you rate the strength of your faith? Your knowledge of the Catholic faith? Your practice of your Catholic faith?

Recommended Resources

For you: Finding a few minutes to take a break in the day can be difficult when we are moving from one thing to another. Loyola Press has you covered! Its three-minute retreats invite you to take a short break on your computer or phone. The Three-Minute Retreat app is free and brings you a new retreat each day in English or Spanish. You can find it in your app store.

For your children: How about a Catholic video game? *Wanderlight: A Pilgrim's Adventure* is a highly immersive, fully narrated game experience that encourages players to travel through three quest-filled realms to explore, to pray, to do good works, and to learn key aspects of the Catholic faith. It is best suited for children between the ages of 5 and 12.

2

Back to Basics with the Holy Three: God, Jesus, and the Holy Spirit

As we discussed in the previous chapter, it's incredibly important to have well-reasoned responses to questions about faith, especially in the "show me" and "prove it" culture we live in today. In a world that shows increasing evidence of religious illiteracy, as believers, knowing and living our faith takes on a new urgency. While it's easy to get lost in the labyrinth of the Catholic Church's teachings and doctrines, it's important to clarify the central tenets of our faith. Misinformation abounds, especially online. Despite what you think your child may understand about the basics of faith, let's take some time to check in with them.

From a base of understanding you can determine any gaps and fill in some of them using the information in this chapter as a guide. It's normal for children's questions to jump from one issue to another, and that's OK as long as they get the foundations. Knowledge and understanding build upon one another, and questions that are hard now will become much more difficult for you to answer at a later age if the underlying principles are not strong. Developing a relationship with the Trinity—God, Jesus, and the Holy Spirit—is at the root of our faith, and unless we clarify some basic information about the who behind the what, then the what and the how of our faith can be difficult to make sense of. In the Bible, we are reminded that these principles are like "storing up . . . treasure" for ourselves as "a good foundation for the future" (1 Tim. 6:19).

You might feel intimidated as you recognize gaps in your own understanding of the faith. But here's a quick story for encouragement!

My friend Father Dan drew frequently on his experience coaching a high school wrestling team when he talked about growing in faith. While he was an athlete himself, he had never actually wrestled competitively. Many people asked him what his strategy was going to be in the absence of personal experience in competitive wrestling. He told me: "I know some basic principles that will transfer to wrestling pretty easily, but my main strategy is to stay one step ahead of the team in understanding and in coaching. I just need to stay one step, one page ahead in the manual. This allows me to be responsive and flexible." Well, it seems that this strategy was a good one. It allowed him to coach a very successful team that went on to win many tournaments. This story is a good reminder to all of us: let's not be afraid to address our children's questions because we don't know all the answers. Read a little bit more about your faith, learn a little bit more, pray a lot more, and stay one step ahead.

What is the Trinity?
—Oliver, age 12

The Trinity is a communion of three persons (God the Father, Jesus Christ, and the Holy Spirit) in one. We are baptized into this mystery, and every time we make the sign of the cross, we express our belief in the Trinity: "In the name of the Father, and of the Son, and of the Holy Spirit. Amen." The word *name* here is critical. It means that we can know the person behind the name.

We might think of it this way. Our ultimate destination and home is with God, who created us and everything else. But God chose to be more than our creator; Jesus instructed us to call God our Father, which means that God intends a quite personal relationship with us, as close as a parent to a child.

Jesus put "skin on God" by becoming one of us, at once fully human and embodying the divine character of God. Through Jesus we could see up close God's character, God's love for us.

The Holy Spirit always existed—the Trinity is eternal—but when Jesus finished his time on earth, the Holy Spirit took on the very personal role of living within us, to teach us God's ways, to give us courage, comfort, wisdom, and guidance.

Who is God?
—Amelia, age 6

Children often ask, "What is God?" It's important to emphasize, as with all members of the Trinity, that God is not an it but a who. Reframing the question in that way is the first step in creating awareness that God can be known and loved. Using personal language when we speak about God helps others relate better to God as a person rather than an impersonal force.

The simple answer is that God is the one who created all of life. God is love. God is the author and source of life. For older children, you can go into more detail, reminding them that our Catholic faith is founded on relationships. We live out our faith in relationship to God, to each other, and to the wider world around us. God is not an impersonal God who sets life in motion from afar but rather one who stays close to the people he loves. There is a vital and living relationship between God and us, the people he loves.

One of the first things we learn about in the Bible is that God is a creator and an artist. God created the Earth from a formless void, and order was brought forth from the chaos of nothingness. The motivation for creation came from the very essence of God, which is goodness and love.

Who is Jesus?

—Eric, age 4

God chose to make himself known to us through the mystery of the Incarnation, when God literally became flesh and became one of us. Jesus' mission was to bring us all into greater relationship with God, who is our Father. Jesus was a real person.

Teenagers will often question this. "But how do we actually know that Jesus was a real person and not just made up?" John, one of my tenth-grade students asked. "I mean, I know what the Bible says about Jesus, but do we have any other credible evidence?" It is important to note that many young people are skeptical of authorities in general, whether political, civil, or religious. Youth ministers have told me that young people increasingly will not accept Jesus based on the word of the Church, but they will accept the Church based on the word of Jesus, the witness of their peers, and our own witness as parents. Leading with the "who" of Jesus rather than the "what" of the Catholic Church for older children can be the first step in helping them come to a relationship with Christ.

The temptation when faced with a question like this is to offer a standard response, such as "Well, the Catholic Church teaches us that Jesus is the only beloved Son of God, our Father." While certainly true, this approach is unlikely to satisfy the hunger behind the question.

For older students, pointing out credible primary sources such as the Jewish historian Josephus and the Roman historian Tacitus can be helpful here. The Romans kept meticulous records, and those records underscore the point that Jesus was a well-documented historical figure. But that is not all. Jesus existed in history, but he also existed before human history and he exists eternally. His point in coming to Earth was to save us from sin so that we, too, can live eternally and with him forever. Jesus saves us from ourselves and the choices we make that go against the abundant life God offers us. These actions are called sins. A sin is any choice that goes against God's love. Sin is how we say no to God.

"Would you die for something that you did not believe in?" I asked John and my tenth-grade class. Not one student said they would.

"I want you to imagine," I said, "that you were at the scene of your friend's death. You witness with your own eyes the murder of one you love. You also, unbelievable as it sounds, meet your friend again—only now he is alive, resurrected. You rush out to tell others about all you've witnessed—the murder and also the resurrection. People look at you like you are crazy. Then one day, you are arrested and condemned to death because you have been telling everyone about your friend, a friend you knew personally. Would you have the courage to die for that truth, or would you lie and live out your days filled with bitterness and regret?"

The apostles were faced with the choice of either living out the message of Jesus every day and bringing him alive to others or denying him and living a lie. When I share with my students that all but one of the apostles was violently killed—beheaded, stoned to death, crucified, and, in the case of Peter, crucified upside down—they are amazed. Why would the apostles allow themselves to be martyred for Jesus rather than deny him? It would have been easier to deny Jesus and deny what they had seen. But they had personal experience of Jesus and his friendship, love, and power. This knowledge of him made it possible for them to die rather than lie. Because, as one of my students answered at the end of the class, "Jesus is really the way, the truth, and the life," just as it says in John 14:6.

Bingo!

Parent to Parent

Question: Do young children have the capacity for a relationship with Jesus?

—*Javier and Gloria, parents of one*

Answer: Yes, children have a very real capacity to understand and develop a relationship with Jesus. Let me share this story with you. When my daughter was 3 years old, she could be a bit of a challenge at Mass. Coming forward to receive Holy Communion, for example, was always interesting. She would accompany me and wave and smile at people and whisper little greetings to her friends along the way. One Sunday, as I was kneeling in prayer after communion, she asked me if Mass was almost over. I replied that very soon we would sing one more song, say goodbye to Jesus, and go home. She then darted into the middle of the aisle, kneeled for a few moments, and began to wave at the altar. Our pastor saw her and waved back. At the top of her voice she loudly exclaimed, "Not you, not you! I am saying goodbye to Jesus before we go home!" Despite the interruption, we all smiled, and it gladdened us to know that in our daughter's heart Jesus is as real to her as the people she sees before her. Oh, that we would all approach Jesus with the same childlike simplicity and trust!

—*Wayne and Julianne, parents of three*

Who is the Holy Spirit?
—*Kyle, age 9*

Questions about God and Jesus are common, but questions about the Holy Spirit are less common. When I ask people, "Which member of the Trinity do you pray to the most: God, Jesus, or the Holy Spirit?" most people respond "God" or "Jesus"; rarely do I hear a reference to the Holy Spirit. The Holy Spirit is the third person of the Trinity. From the ancient Greek philosophers comes the word *pneuma*, which means "breath of life." Derived from the elements of air and fire, *pneuma* is the very spirit or soul of the human person. That word today is the root of words used in many different contexts; pneumatic tires, for example, are filled with air. As Christians, the breath of God *is* the Holy Spirit. Often called "the forgotten God," the Holy Spirit fills us with courage, consoles us in times of trouble, and puts fire in our bellies! In earlier times (and in some early translations of Scripture), the Holy Spirit was called the Holy Ghost, which comes from the Old English word for spirit: *gast*. Each of us is called to be a spirit-fueled Christian, a person filled with the warmth and fire of the Holy Spirit.

Without the Holy Spirit, we would lack spirit: it is the Holy Spirit who shakes us up and gives us the zeal and motivation to share our faith with the world. I have a friend who lives in India, and he reminded me that what we call faith formation or religion class in the Catholic Church is called "animation class" in his culture. It is because the Holy Spirit is the one who enlivens and animates us and the church. Think about that word *animation*. We are animated and brought to life by the Holy Spirit, who directs the mission of the Catholic Church.

What is faith?
—*Madison, age 11*

In any relationship we are free to accept or reject the relationship, and the same is true of faith. Faith is our response to God and a free gift that is given to us. Faith, then, is a belief and trust in God. Living a life of faith means saying yes to God in our daily actions, just as the Blessed Mother Mary did. This *yes* is called our personal adherence to faith. But the *Catechism of the Catholic Church* (*CCC*), which is a collection of the wisdom of the Catholic Church, remarks that "no one can believe alone, just as no one can live alone. You have not given yourself faith as you have not given yourself life" (*CCC* #166). Faith is personal, but it also has a communal dimension because it is lived out in reference to God, others, and the society in which we find ourselves.

The fundamental truths of our faith are expressed in the creed, which I have included in the summary section at the end of this chapter. The word *creed* comes from the Latin word *credo* and means "I believe." Both the Apostles' Creed and the Nicene Creed are considered "professions of faith" because they summarize the basic beliefs of Christianity. In short, the creed is the summary of our faith. When we pray the creed—"I believe in one God, the Father almighty . . . in one Lord, Jesus Christ, the only Begotten Son of God . . . in the Holy Spirit, the Lord, the giver of life"—we are saying that we give our heart to God: Father, Son, and Holy Spirit.

Whew! This has been a lot of ground to cover, but this foundation is necessary to build upon for the coming chapters. Let's now go deeper into learning about the Catholic Church, the saints, and the Blessed Mother.

Take It Home

Key Takeaways

- We are disciples of a *person*. The name of that person is Jesus.
- Speak of "who," not "it." For instance, the Holy Spirit is a person.
- Every friendship takes an investment of time and energy.
- The Holy Spirit is the soul of the church and directs the church's mission.
- God is love and created us out of love.
- The essential truths of our faith are expressed in the creed.

Reflect and Journal

One of the titles for the Holy Spirit is "Paraclete" from the Greek term, *parakletos*, meaning one who advocates, comforts, and comes to our aid. Sometimes we feel burnt out and overwhelmed. The Holy Spirit has been sent to each of us to renew our minds and hearts. Can you identify a time when the Holy Spirit advocated and comforted you?

A Reflection on My Relationship with the Holy Trinity

Questions	Reflect
To whom do I pray most often: God the Father, Jesus Christ, or the Holy Spirit? Why?	
With which member of the Holy Trinity do I have the strongest relationship? Why?	
With which member of the Holy Trinity do I need to develop a stronger relationship? Why?	
Do I invite the presence of the Holy Spirit into my life? Why or why not?	
Our God is a God of love. How does God show his love for me?	
What is my image of Jesus? How does he make his presence known to me?	
The Holy Spirit is known as the Paraclete, meaning "he who is called to one's side," often translated as "consoler." Where in my life do I need consolation?	

Practice: Praying from the Heart, as Taught by Bishop David G. O'Connell

Ask for the Holy Spirit's guidance, light, and life when you are afraid or need help. Introduce your children to this simple exercise.

Take a deep breath. Breathe in and breathe out. Take nice, deep breaths. Pay attention to your breath, notice its rhythm, and breathe slowly in and slowly out.

Invite the Holy Spirit to be with you. Pray the words "Come, Holy Spirit" or another prayer and then rest in God's presence. Asking the Holy Spirit to guide you, begin with your head and move down through each part of your body. Think about your day and picture any tension that is being held in your body. Pay attention to the small aches and pains in all parts of your body, particularly in your fingers, for example, and the tension behind your eyes. Feel them unbinding and unknotting, and then move on to a different part of your body.

Ask the Holy Spirit where you might be holding on to tension and to release this tension. As you visualize your heart, feel your breath expand your heart with love, the love of God. Feel your heart expanding as you breathe in. Picture your heart like a balloon that inflates with your breath, which is filled with love, and then exhale. When you breathe out, imagine yourself breathing out all negativity and criticism. Do this breathing prayer until you have moved through your entire body. Rest in God's presence, and when you are ready, slowly open your eyes.

Pray: Read Slowly the Apostles' Creed

I believe in God, the Father almighty, Creator of heaven and earth; and in Jesus Christ, His only Son, our Lord: Who was conceived by the Holy Spirit, born of the Virgin Mary; suffered under Pontius Pilate, was crucified, died and was buried. He descended into hell; the third day he rose again from the dead; he ascended into heaven, and is seated at the right hand of God the Father almighty; from there he will come to judge the living and the dead. I believe in the Holy Spirit, the holy catholic Church, the communion of saints, the forgiveness of sins, the resurrection of the body, and life everlasting.
Amen.

Recommended Resources

For you: Faith Moves, by Loyola Press. This practical, simple, and engaging little booklet provides opportunities for parents to have faith conversations followed by a complementary game or activity. Designed for all ages.

For your children: Released in 2007, the movie *The Nativity Story* explores the birth of Jesus Christ through the eyes of Mary and Joseph. Over the two years before the birth of Jesus, as Mary realizes that she will bear a child fated to change the world, she discovers the inner strength, faith, and grace that have earned her the veneration of billions of people for two thousand years. Rated PG, the movie can be watched by the whole family. It also provides an authentic depiction of what life was like for Jews in Palestine at that time.

3

Back to Basics:
The Catholic Church, Religion,
Mary, and the Saints

"Sometimes there's nothing basic about the basics," my friend Pam once said to me. She wasn't talking about faith but fashion and how "basics" are the foundation of any good wardrobe! We could say the same about the basics of our faith. Having a foundational understanding of the people at the center of our faith—God the Father, Jesus Christ the Son, and the Holy Spirit—naturally leads us to talk about the Catholic Church, religion, Mary, and the saints. In this chapter, we address some of the specific ways children have asked questions about these basic areas.

What is the Catholic Church? Mass?
—Theresa, age 10

The word that Jesus used for church comes from the Greek word *ekklēsia*, meaning "to call out of," indicating a gathering or assembly, usually for religious purposes. The English word *church* and the German word *Kirche* are both derived from a similar Greek term, *kyriake*, which means "what belongs to the Lord."

When you hear people talk about "the church," listen for three ways this word is used.

1. The liturgical assembly, such as when we "go to church," meaning "we go to Mass."
2. The local community we are a part of; also called our parish.
3. The universal church, the Catholic Church around the world, of which we are a part.

All three of these meanings are interconnected and inseparable. It is in the church where many of the most important moments of our lives take place. Here we, as God's people, are brought to new birth in baptism through water and the Holy Spirit (John 3:5) and to eternal life in the Body and Blood of his Son in the Eucharist (John 6:54). It is in the Church that we confess our sins and our desire to be reconciled to God in the Sacrament of Reconciliation and where we marry our husband or wife or become ordained to be a deacon or a priest. As my friend David tells his fifth-grade students: "Just as you cannot have a king without a kingdom or a body without a head, Jesus is the head and king of the Catholic Church. His kingdom is this world and eternity." Jesus Christ is most powerfully encountered within this community of faith that we call the church.

Western culture particularly emphasizes the values of independence, self-determination, and personal freedom. These values are good to have and are parts of our developing as people. But culture has exalted these values at the expense of understanding the bonds that hold us together—our interdependence and interconnectedness. In reality we are dependent on and connected to so many people throughout our lives. We rely on medical personnel from birth to death. We count on other drivers to be attentive and safe as we share the road with them. We depend on farmers to grow food and essential personnel to keep society moving. So too on our journey of faith do we depend on a community to help us to grow spiritually. This community is the Catholic Church.

At a time when many people, especially young adults, struggle with community life and relationships, Catholicism offers a compelling vision that calls us out of our desire to live solitary lives so that we can live the words of Jesus: "Just as I have loved you, you also should love one another" (John 13:34). Each of us is a part of a community of believers that has survived two thousand years of triumph and tragedy, war and persecution. God has given to each of us the gift of a family in his Church, the Body of Christ, because he knows how much we need one another to live out the life Jesus calls us to live, a life he demonstrated for us. Jesus reminds us that "if one member suffers, all suffer together with it; if one member is honored, all rejoice together with it" (1 Cor. 12:26).

The church is a community of faith gathered to praise and honor God from whom all blessings flow. Once the Mass ends, it is then our work begins as we go forth into the world to share our love of Christ with others.

What's a sacrament?
—Ralph, age 13

We mark important passages of our lives with special items and ceremonies. For example, we have a wedding and exchange wedding rings when we get married. In some cultures, children are given baptismal mugs or cups as a part of their Sacrament of Baptism. Years later, we can look at these precious items and remember the day we got married or had our child baptized. When these moments are celebrated in the Church, there's something even more important happening: God is at work and is most powerfully present in the sacraments. Let's start with the official definition of a sacrament according to the *Catechism of the Catholic Church:* "The sacraments are efficacious signs of grace, instituted by Christ and entrusted to the Church, by which divine life is dispensed to us" (*CCC* #1131).

What does this mean in ordinary terms? A sacrament is a visible sign of God's love for us, and it connects us to God in a powerful way. Think of the sacraments as channels of grace that help God communicate with us through special or extraordinary rituals and actions. For example, baptism marks our formal reception into the Catholic Church. "To baptize" means to immerse in water. Baptism immerses us in the life of God the Father, God the Son, and God the Holy Spirit; it brings us into the community of faith. Through baptism we become part of Jesus' life, death, and resurrection, and we claim a new identity as his beloved sons and daughters. A baptized person is marked indelibly—or invisibly—forever for Christ. Water is the primary symbol for baptism, as we see in the Bible where John the Baptist used water (Matt. 3:11; Mark 1:8a; John 1:33, 3:23), as did Jesus (John 3:22). The water symbolizes the cleansing of sin and the purification into new life. Sacraments are not celebrated in private but in public because we experience grace not merely as individuals but as the family of God. Sacraments make our faith visible, and the community of faith is there to witness them.

What are the Catholic sacraments?
—*Jennifer Lynn, age 14*

There are seven sacraments given to us by Christ. They are Baptism, Confirmation, Holy Eucharist, Reconciliation, Anointing of the Sick, Holy Orders, and Matrimony. Catholic sacraments are divided into three groups: sacraments of initiation (Baptism, Eucharist, and Confirmation), sacraments of healing (Reconciliation and Anointing of the Sick), and sacraments of service (Matrimony and Holy Orders). Each group addresses a unique spiritual need in our lives. For example, in the Catholic Church, marriage is the sacrament whereby a man and woman express their love, commitment, and service to each other through a public marriage ceremony in which they exchange rings and speak vows.

Sacraments coincide with the most important events in life, times when God reaches into our lives and reminds us of his presence in signs and symbols. Years later we can still draw upon the power of these times, especially when we go through a difficult time. Most people can still remember how special they felt during these times. I remember seeing my daughter's face when she put on her dress for her first Holy Communion; the dress was the outward sign of something very powerful—her readiness to receive the gift of the Eucharist and Jesus' presence. On days when she complains about Mass, I remind her of that first time and how special it felt for her to receive Jesus. Perhaps we would approach the sacraments differently if we approached them with the same sense of excitement and anticipation as we did the first time. Perhaps we would come to appreciate them much more deeply if we understood that it might be our last time receiving them.

What's religion?
—*Luis, age 17*

The root of *religion* is *lig*, which comes from Latin and means "to bind or tie together." The word *religion* comes from the Latin word *ligare*, which means "to bind together." This is because our religious beliefs and practices are supposed to knit and bind our lives together. When we live out our faith, it should change how we live, how we parent, how we forgive others. Pope Francis in the past has reminded us that there are no "part-time Christians" who can put on or take off faith like a sweater. Instead, religion is the way in which we live out our faith.

Today, unfortunately, the word *religion* has come to be primarily associated with institutional religion and a subject to be taught rather than a way to live our relationship with Jesus Christ. When someone asks, "What religion are you?" usually they are asking if you believe in one of the "big five" systems of religion: Judaism, Christianity, Islam, Buddhism, and Hinduism. Today, however, *religion* and *religious denomination* are used interchangeably, but they are not the same. A religious denomination indicates a subgroup or subcategory within religion. For example, Catholicism is a subcategory within Christianity. Most of us are officially called Roman Catholics. Are there other kinds of Catholics? You bet! See the next answer for more information.

What does the word *Catholic* mean?
—*Mateo, age 16*

The word *catholic* actually means "universal." This term has its origins in Greek in *kata*, meaning "concerning," and *holou*, meaning "whole"—thus "concerning the whole" or universal. Originally this term was applied to all Christians, but now it is exclusively associated with the largest Christian communion, the Roman Catholic Church.

When we say the words "one holy, catholic and apostolic," we are referring to the entire worldwide Church. There are other Catholic churches besides Roman Catholic that also recognize the pope and are in communion with us: the Alexandrian Catholic Church and the Byzantine Catholic Church, to name just two.

What is spirituality?
—*Luna, age 17*

To be a human being is to have a spirit. In general, *spirituality* refers to how humans experience and nurture their relationship with God. Christian spirituality relates to God in and through Jesus Christ. When someone says that they are "spiritual but not religious," often they mean that their spiritual life is important to them, but they want nothing to do with the institutional church.

However, being religious is not in conflict with the spiritual life, and it is important to be clear with our children on this. Religious belief and practices help us grow in friendship with God, Jesus, and the Holy Spirit, thus nourishing our spiritual lives. Just as we talk to our children about their physical, emotional, and mental health, we also should speak with them about their spiritual health.

We might put it this way: spirituality is one person's experience of God and faith. Religion is the larger experience of a whole community bound together by belief and practice.

Parent to Parent

Question: "But I can talk to God anywhere I want; I don't need to be a part of any church to do that!" is something that my 15-year-old son says to me often. This question gnaws at my heart as a mother, and I'm not sure how to respond. What's the best way to answer his question?

—Carrie, single mom of two, ages 13 and 15

Answer: We have a daughter who says the same thing, and we often remind her that this attitude is like wanting to play basketball but not be on the basketball team (she likes to play basketball). It's fine to play basketball by yourself, but after a while it gets lonely and hard to keep going. Church is the same. We need the support of other people also trying to live what the Gospel teaches—we need each other. The other thing we remind our tribe of six kids is that we have 168 hours in a week. Doesn't God deserve one hour a week when we thank him for all he is doing in our lives? Even my 21-year-old can't argue with that one! Also, while it's true that we can talk to God wherever we want, inside of church or outside of church, the honest answer is that it is in the church where we meet God most directly—in the gift of other people and in the gift of the sacraments, particularly the Eucharist. Jesus is right there, waiting for us. We don't just get to "visit Jesus" at Mass, but we get to consume him, to absorb him in our being.

—Gary and Trish, parents of six kids between the ages of 2 and 21

What's the Bible?
—Kaus, age 5

The Bible is a sacred collection of writings or books that the Catholic Church recognizes as divinely inspired, meaning "written by God's inspiration." The Bible was written in two parts—the Old Testament and the New Testament. The Old Testament books are the sacred scriptures of the Jewish faith, while the New Testament books were written by Christians in the first century. So technically the Bible is not one book but a collection of seventy-three books, written in two parts, with forty-six books of the Old Testament and twenty-seven books of the New Testament. In the most basic terms, the Bible is the central book of our faith.

John, widowed father of two teenagers, puts it this way: "BIBLE stands for Basic Instruction before Leaving Earth—that's the acronym I use to teach my kids about the importance of the Bible. No matter your age, background, or what you go through in life, the Bible covers everything—the basics and all the rest."

The Bible is the foundational text for us as Catholics and we can never overemphasize the importance of reading the Bible, which leads me to the next question.

Are we encouraging Catholics to read the Bible now?
—Amyee K, grandmother of twelve

The short answer to this question is yes. Reading the Bible is always to be encouraged, always.

So why the confusion, particularly among older generations?

This confusion has its origin in a period called the Reformation, which began in the 1500s and was marked by religious upheaval across Europe. Up until that time, the Bible had been written in Latin or Greek and was not typically available to ordinary people, but because it required study, most people who read it were educated—also not typical for ordinary people at the time. But when the printing press was invented, religious texts became available in the languages that ordinary people spoke. This caused much confusion. In Europe, for example, it was documented that during the Reformation, priests spoke out and urged people to be cautious about reading the Bible in their own language, but this is not the case today.

There's an important distinction between how Catholics and Protestants view the Bible. Protestants believe that the Bible is the supreme and only rule of faith. To their credit, those who are Protestant have always emphasized regular reading of the Bible. But Catholics believe that we receive truth and help from God through the Bible but also through "sacred tradition"—the practices of the church—and "apostolic" tradition, which refers to what we have learned from the original apostles and those who have taken their place generation after generation. This apostolic tradition comes to us in the teaching of those called to be authorities in the Catholic Church—we call these teachers the magisterium. The Church gives them authority to interpret and teach what the Bible gives us in its many stories, wisdom sayings, poetry, history, and accounts of Jesus' life, death, and resurrection. So for us, it is "the church" (remember those three meanings of church we talked about earlier?) and the Bible that help us grow in holiness.

What is holiness?
—Jordan and Kathryn, parents of three

Practicing our faith and growing in our spiritual life is a path to wholeness or, to put it another way, to holiness. It is important to look at the word *holy* in the context in which it is used in the Bible. The word *holy* comes from the Hebrew word *qadosh*. *Qadosh* literally means "to be set apart for a special purpose." To strive for holiness is to recognize that we are set apart by God who created us. The *Catechism of the Catholic Church* reminds us that "all Christians in any state or walk of life are called to the fullness of Christian life and to the perfection of charity. All are called to holiness and one of the best ways to do that is to avoid sin" (*CCC* #2013).

What is a sin?
—Bryan, age 6

The topic of sin can be hard to address, especially with children who may worry about the consequences of their actions. This can be even more complicated to talk about with children who have a disability. Nick from Kentucky indicates that some of his family members are neurodivergent: he has four children who have been diagnosed with various combinations of autism and ADHD. "My oldest son is high anxiety, so he's pretty regularly asking me if certain actions are sins or not. I have to find the balance between telling him the truth and reassuring him that he's a good person and that, with Jesus, he doesn't have to worry," says Nick.

Remember, the heart of our Catholic faith is relationship—with God and with one another. Because God loves us so much, he gives us free will, which is the ability to choose for ourselves whether to love God or to reject him. God will never impose faith upon anyone but allows us to choose for ourselves our own course of action. Many times, through our actions we have turned from God and refused to admit our failures and wrongdoing. We hurt ourselves, hurt those we love, and damage our relationship with God. When you are in a relationship with someone and you continuously hurt them, your relationship becomes broken. Our relationship with God is broken because of sin. A sin is any choice that goes against God's love. Sin is how we say no to God. The word *sin* comes from the Greek word *hamartia* or the Hebrew word *hata*. Both words mean "to miss the mark" or "flawed."

Initially, *sin* was a term used in archery or spear throwing when someone missed the target. For us as Christians, sin is any action or behavior that damages our relationships with God and other people. There are two types of sin—venial sin and mortal sin.

A mortal sin is the most serious of all sins and represents a grave and deliberate turning away from God. Those who commit mortal sin must have full knowledge of the weight or gravity of the sin and consent to the sin. Serious examples of mortal sins include murder, participating in genocide, and abortion.

Venial sins are less serious sins that weaken our union with God and are often committed without full knowledge of how they harm our relationship with God. All sin is to be avoided, however, whether mortal or venial.

Fortunately, we can reconcile with God and confess our sins through the Sacrament of Reconciliation, or what is also known as confession, which we cover in a later chapter.

Who is Mary?

—Logan and Laura, twins, age 8

As parents we know our children better than anyone, and Mary, as Jesus' mother, can teach us so much about Jesus. God could have entered the world in any way he wanted, but God chose one of us, a humble woman, to be the one who bore Jesus. Mary as the Mother of Jesus is also the Mother of God because God and Jesus are one and the same. She holds a special place in the Catholic Church as the first and best disciple. It was from Mary and Joseph that Jesus learned to pray, to be obedient to God, and to honor the commandments. As St. Mother Teresa put it so simply: "Know Mary, know Jesus; no Mary, no Jesus." If we know Mary, we can know Jesus better too.

One of the trickiest things to talk to children about is a very human point, that Mary was a virgin when she conceived Jesus. This conception was made possible through the Holy Spirit, but helping children understand this can be tough. Many parents find themselves saying, "But it's a mystery!"—so much that children can start to tune us out if we don't engage in a solid conversation about this point. Young children can accept that God chose Mary because she was special and that might be as far as you need to go with the conversation. For older children, though, who are beginning to understand biology and reproduction, this conversation can be challenging to navigate well. Here's how Joan, mother of two, handled it:

> When my kids got into middle school, many of their classroom units that touched on sexuality made for a barrage of questions. When my daughter asked me how it was possible for Mary to conceive Jesus as a virgin, I knew that this was an opportunity for us to talk about chastity, purity, and sexuality in relation to our own lives and then apply this to Mary. A friend talked with me about this before I had the conversation and reminded me that the story of the Annunciation would be helpful to talk about. I got out my Bible and we read this together. The Annunciation is the first time that we hear Mary speak in the Bible in response to the angel Gabriel. We talked about the phrase "full of grace" especially because that phrase indicates Mary's sinlessness. I can't say that this was an easy conversation, but opening the Bible together was the beginning of several more conversations. I would also say for parents wanting to have this conversation with their children, my advice would be for moms to talk about it first with their daughters and dads with their sons so you can talk about some of the bodily and sexuality issues from your own perspective. I did this first with my daughter and then we all talked about it together afterward.

As Catholics, we profess a belief in the doctrine of the immaculate conception. A doctrine is a truth that the church teaches is necessary for us to accept. Mary was conceived without sin so that she could be the immaculate vessel for the conception of her son, Jesus Christ. The angel Gabriel at the moment of the Annunciation salutes her as "full of grace." This title comes from the Greek word *kecharitomene*, which describes a superabundance of grace. In Ireland this is translated as *lan de ghrasta.*

But Mary herself did not inherit sin, nor did she sin throughout her life. Many Catholics are asked if we pray "to" Mary, often by those from other Christian denominations such as Lutherans and Methodists, and the short answer is no. However, this question deserves a bit more exploration, so we tackle it in our upcoming chapter on prayer.

What is a saint?
—Francis, age 14

"Thanks, you're a saint!" might be a common enough reply when someone has done something nice for us, but becoming a saint is far more difficult. While all of us are called to holiness, the saints are those who lived extraordinary lives of holiness, often under great pressure or demanding conditions. The fruit of their lives resulted in miracles confirmed with "signs and wonders and mighty works" (2 Cor. 12:12). These miracles were the fruit of their faithfulness and devotion to God. The process for being named a saint in the Catholic Church is called *canonization.* This process affirms the person's life as being worthy of "heroic virtue," and the person is listed in the "canon," or the authoritative listing of the saints. As such, a saint is often given his or her own day, a "feast day." For example, St. Patrick of Ireland's feast day is March 17, which is commonly thought to be the day that he died. St. Martín de Porres's feast day is November 3, also thought to be the day he died. Reading the lives of the saints, celebrating specific feast days, and asking for the intercession (prayerful help) of saints can be an important way to help remind children that sainthood is something to which all of us are called. Talk about the saints with your children in a way that can inspire them to sainthood too. The saints were real people! Blessed Carlo Acutis (3 May 1991–12 October 2006) designed a website and loved to play video games. He also loved to attend Mass and pray the rosary. When he died, he was buried in his Nike sneakers, and his faith inspires millions of people around the world. Sainthood is within the reach of all of us who desire to live a life of holiness!

What's a disciple? What's an apostle?
—*Martha, age 19*

We are disciples of a person, and that person is Jesus Christ. Quite simply, a disciple is a friend and follower of Jesus. The word *disciple* comes from the Greek word *mathetes,* meaning a pupil or student of the master. The master is, of course, Jesus Christ. A disciple is one who follows Jesus, loves him, desires to learn from him, be with him, and share him with others. The identity of a disciple springs from Jesus Christ, through faith and baptism, and grows in the church, our community of faith. In the Bible the first people Jesus called were simply called "the disciples," as we learn in the Gospel according to Luke 6:13–16: "And when day came, he called his disciples and chose twelve of them, whom he also named apostles: Simon, whom he named Peter, and his brother Andrew, and James, and John, and Philip, and Bartholomew, and Matthew, and Thomas, and James son of Alphaeus, and Simon, who was called the Zealot, and Judas son of James, and Judas Iscariot, who became a traitor." These men became known as the apostles as Jesus' public ministry progressed, and they are first called apostles in Matthew 10:2. The word *apostle* means "messenger or one who is sent." The apostles are those who are sent out in the name of the church. Along with St. Paul, who was not originally one of the twelve, the apostles were called and sent out into the world to "go therefore and make disciples" (Matt. 28:19). Today, we use the term *disciple* to refer to anyone who wants to follow Jesus Christ more closely.

Take It Home

Key Takeaways

- There are three ways that the word *church* is used: (1) the liturgical assembly such as when we "go to church," meaning we "go to Mass"; (2) the local community that we are a part of, or, our parish; and (3) the universal church—the wider Catholic Church around the world, of which we are a part.
- We are all called to a life of holiness, which includes participating in the sacraments, avoiding sin, and following Jesus Christ.
- A disciple is someone who strives to follow Jesus Christ. Mary our Mother is the first and best disciple.
- Saints are those who lived exemplary lives of holiness.
- The Bible is a sacred collection of writings or books that the Catholic Church recognizes as divinely inspired.
- The word *catholic* means "universal."

Reflect and Journal

I can do all things through him who strengthens me.
—Philippians 4:13

It is never too late to start a new habit such as praying the Scriptures. Whether you go to Mass every week or once a year, have been a part of the church your whole life or have been away for fifty years, it is never too late to take a step toward God in faith. He is waiting for each of us, his beloved children, to come home to him, one day at a time, one step at a time. What one step can you make to grow your faith? What one habit can strengthen your faith for your children?

A Handy Guide to Catholic Words and What They Mean

Word	Meaning	Significance in My Life
Catholic	The word catholic is derived from the Greek *katholikos* which means "universal".	
Church	(1) The liturgical assembly such as when we "go to church," meaning we "go to Mass"; (2) Our parish or local community; (3) The universal Catholic Church around the world.	
Religion	The word religion comes from the Latin word *ligare*, which means "to bind together."	
Spirituality	Spirituality refers to how humans experience and nurture their relationship with God. Christian spirituality relates to God in and through Jesus Christ.	
Holy	To strive for holiness is to recognize that we are set apart by God who created us.	
Sin	Early words for sin mean "to miss the mark" or "flawed."	
Apostle	The word apostle means "messenger" or "one who is sent out."	
Disciple	A disciple is a friend and follower of Jesus.	

Practice: Easy Method for Reading Scripture

Read the Scriptures using the format "read, reflect, pray, rest." It works like this: read a little bit of Scripture, reflect upon what it means, pray a response from your heart, and then rest in God's presence. This is a simplified version of what is called *lectio divina*, or prayerful reading, which we address in a later chapter.

Pray: The Hail Mary

Pray the Hail Mary by meditating on the life of the Blessed Mother:

Hail Mary, full of grace, the Lord is with thee,
Blessed art thou among women and blessed is the fruit of thy womb Jesus.
Holy Mary, Mother of God, pray for us sinners,
now and at the hour of our death.
Amen.

Recommended Resources

For you: Far too many Catholics think of the saints as old, cold, and irrelevant to everyday life. Bob Burnham, however, experiences the saints as something quite different: beautiful examples of people who, though flawed like us, opened themselves to God's grace and can teach us to do the same. In *Little Lessons from the Saints: 52 Simple and Surprising Ways to See the Saint in You*, Burnham skips the typical biographies of saints and offers instead brief but powerful spiritual lessons from fifty-two different saints, each followed by a short meditation.

For your children: Try *The Garden, the Curtain and the Cross Storybook: The True Story of Why Jesus Died and Rose Again*, by Carl Lafteron. This book for children ages 3–6 explains the basic story of the life, death, and resurrection of Jesus, including the reality of sin.

4

Making Mass Count: Surviving and Thriving at Mass

"But I don't get very much out of Mass these days," Matt, a father of four said to me. "The kids are noisy; someone always has to go to the bathroom, and once or twice a parishioner has given us 'the eye' because the children move around quite a bit," he said. "My wife and I feel like we're both so distracted doing crowd control during Mass that we barely hear the homily. Wouldn't it be easier to stay at home?"

"Yes," I said, "easier, but not better." Matt chuckled at that. After talking for some time, Matt concluded: "Like anything in life, I suppose, anything that's worth doing well is often hard. Anyway, it won't be like this forever." He added, "We'll continue by braving the wild frontier of Mass and put it all in God's hands."

Let's be honest: at one time or another we have all had the same thought—it's just too hard to take the family to Mass, so maybe we should stay home, especially when our children are small. We rationalize that we are too tired for Mass or that our fellow parishioners aren't the friendliest at times. But we also know that taking our children to Mass is essential and the cornerstone of our Catholic faith. In this chapter, we address some common questions related to the Mass and provide information, insights, and tips from other parents that can help you and your family not just survive but thrive at Mass.

Why do we have to go to Mass?

—Imani, age 16

Sound familiar? While this is one of the most common questions we hear as parents, it's often the most difficult to answer. So why do we as Catholics go to Mass? Let's start with how Janette and Kevin, parents of five, answered this question.

> Our answer to this question evolved as our children got older. The timeless answer was, "Because we need Jesus, in the Eucharist, to get us through the week. Jesus loves you and wants you there with Him." As they started school and noticed that not all their friends were at Mass, we stressed, "Different families have different traditions, and Sunday Mass is one important way that we spend time together as a family." All our children were so excited to receive their first communion, and often kept count of their second, third, fourth, and so on. Around middle school years, they needed reminding, "We go to church to receive the sacraments." When those answers were no longer detailed enough, then: "Sunday Mass keeps us centered on Jesus. All week we are influenced by non-Christian friends, coworkers, teachers, and media. Some weeks are worse than others, but we are being drawn slowly away from Jesus, so gradually sometimes that we don't even realize it. We need to hear his message weekly to keep us on the right track. We need Jesus to work inside us, through his Body and Blood, to guide us on the path to heaven. The longer we stay away, the further we will drift and the harder it will be to return to his grace." We would always follow up any of these responses by sharing that we—*Mom and Dad*—also need Jesus, *we* need the sacraments, and *we* need to recenter ourselves after being influenced by the stresses of day-to-day life. It was never just that *they* needed to go to church. We always admitted that we needed to go too.

What Janette's thoughtful response reminds us of is that attending Mass is at the heart of our Catholic faith. Let's review some basic information you and your family can talk about as you discuss Mass.

Sunday is that special day of the week when our whole Catholic community comes together throughout the world to give honor and glory and praise to God. For Catholics, Mass is not simply the end of the week, but traditionally it has always been considered the first day of the week. This is an important point: Mass isn't something we do at the end of the week, after we do everything else during the week; it is the beginning of the week so that we can begin our week with putting God first in our lives.

Sunday is the one day when we especially rejoice in the gift of the Eucharist, which is one of the earliest terms for the Mass. The word *Eucharist* means "thanksgiving." We give thanks for all the blessings we have received in the past week and ask God for his blessings on the week ahead. We stand with our family, friends, and neighbors to receive a taste of heaven, right on this earth! Every time we participate in the celebration of the Eucharist, we renew our belief in the truth that Christ gave his very life for each of us and that we are redeemed by his life, death, and resurrection. The Eucharist is the most powerful way in which Jesus Christ is present to us because he is fully present in the Eucharist. We call this the "Real Presence of Christ in the Eucharist."

While the Catholic Church teaches that it is a sin to miss Mass except for a serious or grave reason, and we are obliged to go to Mass every Sunday and on holy days of obligation, there are Catholics who go to Mass out of a sense of obligation rather than love. One way to talk with children about this is to remind them of how they spend time with people they love. Remember earlier when we talked about faith as relationship? Brock puts it this way when he talks to his third-grade students at the Catholic school where he teaches: "Going to

Mass is an act of love, where we tell God just how much we love him, and we allow him to pour his love into us as well in the Eucharist. To worship and praise him is an act of love. We don't want to go to Mass because we are told to, but instead because we want to."

We go to Mass to receive but also to share. At the end of Mass (called the dismissal), we are sent forth renewed to share our faith with the world. We are sent on mission. The final words of the Mass in Latin are *Ite, missa est*—which, roughly translated, means "Go, it is sent." From *missa* we derive many other English words such as *Mass, dismissal, mission, commission.* Our mission is to share with the world what we have been given.

In addition to the information above, take the time to think about your own specific reason for going to Mass. On days when you feel like skipping out, what keeps you coming to Mass? You can explain to your children the reasons for going to Mass, but your own personal witness to why you attend Mass is likely to have the biggest impact upon your children.

Parent to Parent

Question: How can I help my child to understand that Jesus isn't just for Sunday?

—Lawrence and Tina, parents of one

Answer: My husband's grandmother, Anna, had a ready smile for everyone, and within constant reach of her gnarled hands were her well-worn rosary beads. Anna's hands were a map of the life she had lived—hands that worked the earth as she tended her garden, hands that kneaded bread, hands that threaded fishing hooks onto fishing line, and hands that she folded in prayer throughout the day. She was cared for with great devotion by her granddaughter for many years until Anna's mind became lost in the thick fog of Alzheimer's disease. Finally, and with great sadness, the family made the decision to have Anna placed in care because of her increasing medical needs.

To Anna's great delight, the care facility was filled with the sounds of Anna's childhood: Polish spoken by the sisters who cared for her and the chimes calling the residents to Mass each morning. My husband and I visited Anna often and always on a Sunday. When the residents would see our family, they would exclaim that it was "visiting day" and perk right up. We loved our time with Anna, but at the end of our visits, we always left feeling sad. Sunday was visiting day. A bittersweet day. A happy-sad day.

For many Catholics today, Sunday has become "visiting day" with Jesus. We come to church, bearing well wishes and snippets of news that we share in our prayers, and we receive the greatest gift of all in the body and blood of Jesus Christ. We may leave content and more at peace, but if we do not speak with Jesus again all week, Sunday does indeed become a kind of "visiting day." It shouldn't be. Jesus is for every day.

—Wayne and Julianne, parents of three

But I don't understand what's happening at Mass! What's going on?
—Chloé, age 13

I want to share a personal moment that transformed how I approached Mass with my children. I wrote about this story in my book *Start with Jesus: How Everyday Disciples Will Renew the Church*, and it continues to resonate with many parents.

It was a Sunday morning when I went to wake Ian, my 3-year-old son, for Mass. "What day is it?" he asked sleepily. "It's Sunday, son, that means it's time for church," I said. Under the blankets I heard an audible sigh of displeasure. And then he said the words that all parents dread: "I don't want to go to Mass." It was the first time I had ever heard him say this, and so I asked him why. In my mind, I thought about all the reasons a child might not want to go to Mass: how few children he would see in our church, the quietness and lack of movement, the fact that he often could not see what was happening, the style of music, the lack of snacks. But my son did not give any of those reasons. "I don't want to go to church, Mama," he whispered, "because nobody looks happy there." Who knows what my 3-year-old saw on the faces of those who were present at the Mass? Perhaps he mistook reverence and solemnity for boredom, or perhaps he mistook boredom for a lack of understanding? What did he see in me as his mother? Am I filled with joy on my way to Mass or rushed and harried trying to get everyone there on time?

Only God knows what was stirring in Ian's little heart, but I do think that his comment points to something we need to be conscious of: what we convey when we participate in the Mass. St. John Vianney, patron saint of parish priests, echoed this connection between joy and understanding when he said, "If we really understood the Mass, we would die of joy." How many of us take the time to really understand what is happening at Mass so that we can be filled with a greater sense of peace, hope, joy, and reverence? If you want your children to understand what's happening at Mass, then you must understand too.

Parent to Parent

Question: What is one practical way to prepare our children for Mass?

—Amir and Destiny, parents of four

Answer: Check their pockets! Let me explain why. With three children under age 7, going to Mass was often a challenge for our family. There were plenty of wiggles and giggles, tears, tantrums, visits to the bathroom, and inappropriate outbursts. But we persevered, and generally people were kind and helpful at our parish. It was at a late evening Saturday Mass when I became aware of a chuckle or two behind our family. When it first happened, I didn't think too much of it, but it increased in frequency at random times, and I worriedly, and discreetly, checked all the children. There were no skirts tucked into underwear, nobody was showing their bellybutton, and everyone seemed to be paying attention. Whew! But then when the chuckles turned into a full-out giggle, I became suspicious that someone in our family was drawing attention to themselves, and I couldn't locate the instigator.

As the Mass progressed, the light outside grew dimmer. In the winter light, we all progressed to receive Holy Communion. Each of the older children was ahead of me, while I held the youngest and my husband held another child. All of a sudden, my daughter turned around and smiled at me! I did a double take. What on earth was in her mouth?! It was the week after Halloween, and my 6-year-old had tucked into her pocket a set of hot-pink glow-in-the-dark vampire teeth. She was smiling at all and sundry when her parents were not looking! We now check the children's pockets each week when we go to Mass.

—*Wayne and Julianne, parents of three*

But why do *we* have to go to Mass?
—*Jonathan, age 14*

"I just don't see why we have to go every Sunday," Carrie's 14-year-old son, Jonathan, said repeatedly. "Jake's family doesn't always go and they're nice people!" This line of questioning sometimes made Carrie feel worn down but also torn. She wanted her children to go to Mass, but she struggled with forcing them to be there and wondered if that would be more harmful in the long term.

As children grow and progress, they become aware of dissonance and tension in many areas of life, including faith. They see their friends going shopping, heading out to sports events, or going to the beach on Sunday instead of going to Mass. If they see their friends in church at Easter and Christmas, for example, but not at other times of the year, it can be confusing, and teenagers may try to wiggle out of going to Mass.

There are two areas that need unpacking in Carrie's situation and that apply to us all: why we go to Mass and how going to Mass benefits us.

We must be careful to respond to the question in such a way that does not unfairly judge the intentions of others. Carrie explains: "I told Jonathan that every family lives out their faith differently. As Catholics, we believe that going to Mass every Sunday is super important, and our family always has and will always put Mass ahead of going to the movies or shopping on a Sunday. I don't know why Jake's family doesn't go to Mass every Sunday, but Jake's family is not our family, and this is what our family does." Carrie and Jonathan then talked about the different ways that going to Mass helped their family, especially as their family had experienced a lot of tragedy. Carrie had lost her husband, Jon, to cancer three years before this conversation and knew that her son was struggling.

This conversation provided an opening for Carrie to share just how important faith was in helping their whole family keep Jon's memory alive. "I think about your father at every Mass," Carrie said as she held her son's hand. "During the prayers of the faithful, we are invited to remember anyone that has died, and I always think of your father." She explained to me: "Mass is the place I take my pain. I know God can handle it and I can handle life a little better after going." While this is undoubtedly a heart-wrenching example, each of us has our own reasons for going to Mass, and we should share some of these reasons (as appropriate) with our children.

For some of us, Mass helps us keep grounded and be more at peace with ourselves and the world. For others, it is a routine that reminds us of our place in life, one among many but loved by Jesus all the same.

Are there any actual benefits to going to Mass?

—Jesse, age 15

Yes! Research is finally confirming what people of faith have always known: taking the time to pray individually has incredible benefits, but so too does engaging in a public community act of worship such as Mass. One study released in 2016 in a journal published by the American Medical Association indicates that those who attend church services generally live longer than people who don't.

Over a twenty-year span, the study surveyed a group of more than seventy-six thousand female nurses, most of whom were Catholic or Protestant. One of their findings indicated that women who went to religious services more than once a week were 33 percent less likely to die prematurely than those who never attended services. This led the study's authors and researchers to a striking recommendation: "Religion and spirituality may be an underappreciated resource that physicians could explore with their patients, as appropriate," they wrote. "Our results do not imply that health care professionals should prescribe attendance at religious services, but for those who already hold religious beliefs, attendance at services could be encouraged as a form of meaningful social participation."

Another study, released in 2018 by the Harvard T. H. Chan School of Public Health, found that children with a religious upbringing benefit physically and mentally, too, especially as young adults. Children who attended Mass weekly or had an active prayer life were more positive and had greater life satisfaction in their twenties than those who did not. These young adults also tended to choose a healthier lifestyle, avoiding drinking, smoking, drug use, and sexual promiscuity. Based on a sample of five thousand children over eight to fourteen years, the study also indicated that at least 18 percent of regular churchgoers reported higher levels of happiness in their twenties than their nonreligious peers. And more importantly, out of the same sample, 29 percent tended to join in community causes, and 33 percent stayed away from illicit drugs.

While it is tempting to simply recite this information, sharing our own witness to the benefits of attending Mass is likely to be just as impactful, and perhaps more impactful, than just listing rote facts.

We should also be mindful about speaking of Mass attendance as "insurance" when it comes to social, emotional, and mental health issues. Having faith and going to Mass don't mean that we won't suffer or go through tough times, and we need to be honest with our children about this. Honesty can help avoid what is called *moral therapeutic deism*, whereby God is reduced to being a therapist and moral guide whom we call upon when we are in difficulty instead of the One who is at the center of our lives. Having faith does not mean that we will not struggle, but it does mean that we will have a foundation for a relationship to sustain us as we endure life's difficulties. If we truly want to live the Mass, then we must understand and participate in it.

So why can't we just watch Mass on TV or the internet?
—*Cassidy, age 12*

It may seem obvious, but watching something on the television or a computer is not the same as experiencing it. Anyone who has been to a live music event understands how different that is from watching it on a screen. There is no substitute for actually experiencing it. The same is true for Mass. During the early days of the COVID-19 pandemic, businesses, schools, and churches closed their doors temporarily, and many Catholic parishes offered livestreaming Mass as an alternative to in-person worship. For many Catholic parishes, this was their first foray into the world of livestreaming Mass; for others, it was already a service they provided in addition to in-person worship.

Regardless, during these early days of the pandemic when in-person worship was not available, parishes employed all the means at their disposal to reach their people and streamed their Masses virtually and digitally. But it is important to remember that this was an extraordinary time for the world and a time when many Catholic dioceses suspended the obligation to attend Mass in person due to the pandemic.

But a livestreamed Mass is no substitute for attending Mass in person with our community of faith. We cannot fully be a part of our parish community and the universal church from the refuge of our couches, as one viral post on Facebook attributed to many different authors suggests:

> As church attendance numbers fade across the nation and online services become very convenient, it's important to remember why church attendance for you and your family matters so much. You can't serve from your sofa. You can't have community of faith on your sofa. You can't experience the power of a room full of believers worshipping together on your sofa.
>
> Christians aren't consumers. We are contributors. We don't watch. We engage. We give. We sacrifice. We encourage. We pray. We do life together.

Sometimes we miss going to Mass because of illness or other family emergency. But simply choosing not to be present in the faith community is not in harmony with what we believe about worship, communal prayer, and the Eucharist.

What happens if you miss Mass?
—*Aria, age 10*

We sometimes forget that what we have freely available to us every day (going to Mass) has been punishable by death at various times in history. Indeed, today in certain parts of the world, it is forbidden and outlawed to be a Christian.

What we take for granted, others would willingly die for. This is a perspective to keep in mind as we approach this issue. So, what happens if you miss Mass? On the surface nothing happens if you or your family miss Mass. But at the level of our souls, quite a lot. The key here is the word *miss*. What are we missing? For one thing, we deprive ourselves of God's very presence in our own bodies: the Eucharist. This weakens us spiritually and makes us less able to withstand the challenges that come our way. Missing Mass means that we miss out on what God wants to offer us in that moment: to live an abundant life filled with joy, peace, and love. Missing Mass means that we do not live as God wants us to live. We also are missing from our family of faith, the Body of Christ. God misses us, and our family of faith misses us even if we don't realize it.

To explain this to a child, it is important to be direct and clear. The Catholic Church teaches that to miss Mass on Sunday without a valid or serious reason is a mortal sin. A mortal sin is the most serious sin of all (venial sins are lesser sins), representing a willful and deliberate turning away from God. For a sin to be mortal, all these conditions or requirements must be met:

1. It must be serious (grave matter).
2. We choose it freely (full consent).
3. We understand the gravity of our choice (full knowledge).

If one of those elements is missing, the act is not a mortal sin. If the three are present, it is a mortal sin. Skipping Mass on Sunday to go shopping when you know the Church's teaching is a serious matter. In this situation, we should go to Mass but only receive the Eucharist after we have sought reconciliation with God in the Sacrament of Reconciliation. While we are always welcome to participate at Mass, the church asks us not to receive the Eucharist with mortal sin on our soul.

Of course, there are serious circumstances that may excuse us from attending Mass, such as if we are sick, if an emergency arises, or if we cannot attend without a real burden such as when there is a blizzard and we cannot get to Mass safely without risk. In these circumstances, we should take the time to pray, read the Scriptures for the week, watch Mass on television, and practice what is called a *spiritual communion*. This means that we can share with God how we want to be close to him in our thoughts, actions, and prayers even if we cannot be physically present. An example of a spiritual communion is listed at the end of this chapter. Part of what we miss when we participate in a livestream is the physical act of consuming the Eucharist, which leads nicely to our next question from Robin.

What does the phrase "Real Presence of Christ in the Eucharist" mean?
—Robin, age 14

When Jesus spoke to the disciples, he used a form of storytelling called a parable. Parables are simple stories that reveal deeper or greater spiritual truths. For example, Jesus compared the Kingdom of God to a mustard seed in Matthew 31:31–32. "The kingdom of heaven is like a mustard seed that someone took and sowed in his field; it is the smallest of all the seeds, but when it has grown it is the greatest of shrubs and becomes a tree, so that the birds of the air come and make nests in its branches." Jesus used parables to explain complex things to his disciples all the time, and in this case, he wanted to show how there are properties of the mustard seed that can teach us about God and his kingdom. However, in Jesus' "bread of life discourse" he used very precise language to describe the Eucharist and its relationship to his body. The bread-of-life discourse is a portion of Jesus' teaching that appears in the Gospel of John 6:22–59. In this discourse Jesus uses clear "I am" statements such as

- "I am the bread of life" (John 6:35).
- "I am the bread that came down from heaven" (John 6:41).
- "I am the living bread" (John 6:51).

Note that Jesus does not use *like* or comparative language here as he does other times in the Gospels. He does not say "I am like the bread of life" but "I *am* the bread of life." His use of "I am" language is highly significant. Jesus implied in his declarations that the Eucharist is his very body (Luke 22:19) and his real presence (John 6:26–65).

As Catholics, we do not believe that the bread and wine are merely symbols of Jesus' body and blood but that they are truly transformed into the real body and blood of Jesus. This is known as the doctrine of *transubstantiation* and is one of the central tenets of our Catholic faith. One of the best ways to prepare yourself and your family for Mass is to talk about the use of language at Mass and what Jesus meant. Listen carefully to the words of the Scriptures and the words of the priest. Good preparation is one of the keys to appreciating what's unfolding at Mass.

How can we prepare ourselves and our children for Mass?

—Sarah and Ryan, parents of two

If you love sports, you have undoubtedly heard the expression from Gene Wolfe that "the best defense is a strong offense." This adage has been applied to sports, military pursuits, and investment strategies. But applied to the Mass, it takes on a new meaning. If we want our children to love the Mass and live out what the Mass means, then we need to prepare accordingly.

Cliff and Erin decided to educate themselves on what was happening at Mass so that they could pass this along to their children organically through the years. "When our children were really little," Cliff explains, "we would take the time during the Mass to whisper into their ears. We would say, 'See, Kaitlyn, see how Father is pouring the wine into a special vessel. This is called a chalice. Watch how he is going to add a little bit of water to mix into the wine. The mixing of the water and the wine signifies a few different things, which we will talk about later.' Then later on at home," Cliff explains, "Erin and I would sit down with the kids and talk to them about specific moments from the Mass. I used to feel a bit uncomfortable whispering into their ears this way, but at times this was really helpful for keeping the kids' attention. As long as we kept things very quiet, it was not disruptive at all."

This was one way that Cliff and Erin helped their children understand the Mass, but there are many other ways to deepen your family's understanding of the Mass depending on the age and receptivity of your children. The "Take It Home" section at the end of this chapter contains some practical ideas shared by other parents.

Take It Home

Key Takeaways

- Sunday Mass is when we give honor and glory and praise to God.
- For Catholics, Mass is not the culmination of the week but traditionally has always been considered the first day of the week.
- We are obliged to go to Mass at least once per week.
- As Catholics, we believe that the bread and wine are truly transformed into the real Body and Blood of Jesus. This is known as the doctrine of transubstantiation and one of the central tenets of our Catholic faith.
- The word *Eucharist* means thanksgiving.

Reflect and Journal

Is going to Mass at the heart of your family? Is there coherence between what you say about your faith and how you live? How can you learn to love the Mass more?

An Overview of the Mass

Name	Parts	How I Experience It
Introductory Rites	Entrance Antiphon	
	Greeting	
	Penitential Act	
	Kyrie	
	Gloria (on Sundays and solemnities only)	
	Collect	
Liturgy of the Word	First Reading	
	Responsorial Psalm	
	Second Reading	
	Gospel Acclamation	
	Homily	
	Profession of Faith, or The Creed, (on Sundays and solemnities only)	
	Universal Prayer (also known as Prayer of the Faithful)	
Liturgy of the Eucharist	Presentation Preparation of the Gifts	
	Prayer over the Offerings	
	Eucharistic Prayer	
	Communion Rite includes the: Lord's Prayer, Sign of Peace, Lamb of God, Distribution of Communion Prayer after Communion	
Concluding Rites	Solemn Blessing	
	Dismissal	

Practice: Make Mass More Meaningful

Here's a compilation of helpful advice from parents.

1. **Prepare for Mass ahead of time.** Tell your children about the Sunday Scriptures ahead of time or on the way to Mass: "We live about ten minutes from church, which was the perfect amount of time to give a summary. On days that we talked about Mass on the way home, we found this pre-Mass introduction helped them understand better the day's readings. Depending on their age, having a book about the Mass they can follow along with or a children's missalette keeps them more engaged."

2. **Set expectations.** Mass attendance should be expected. Janette and Kevin note that just as you require children to "go to school, brush their teeth, or pick up their toys, it should be clear that Sunday Mass is simply something you do every week. A ready response sends a clear message. We feel that at least we did our part by bringing them to the Eucharist, and Jesus could do the rest. If they have a busy weekend coming up, we remind them in advance that they need to make time for Mass. If they have a friend spending the weekend with us, the friend is expected to come to Mass with us even if they are not Catholic."

3. **Sit up front at Mass.** It sounds counterintuitive, but many parents report that sitting up front helped their children feel more comfortable at Mass. For one, children can better see what is happening on the altar. Sitting up front also makes it easier to explain the Mass, and they are not distracted by other people in front of them. By being able to watch the servers, they become more confident and excited to start serving themselves.

4. **Skip the "cry room" or "family room" (unless for specific reasons such as feeding or settling down children who are upset).** "Our parish had a room like this that had a few books, stuffed animals, and one or two quiet toys," notes Janette. "For a toddler, the freedom of being able to walk around and play is way more fun than sitting in the pew! Our kids quickly learned that being loud meant a trip back to the 'fun room.' This was fun for them, but not so fun for us." It is OK to go to the family room to settle down a child, but return to the pew to reinforce that church is prayer time, not play time.

5. **Skip the snacks during Mass.** Skip treats and snacks during Mass unless they are for very little children. Many parents find it more effective to promise a treat after church if the children behave during Mass.

6. **Debrief on the way home.** Ask a few questions: What was the most important thing that you heard today? Was there something that you were curious or had more questions about? What was the Gospel about? What can we keep doing, do differently or better as a result of what we heard today?

7. **Involve them.** Encourage age-appropriate participation such as altar serving, being ministers of hospitality, singing in the choir, helping with the recording technology for the livestream, or reading at Mass.

8. **Keep Mass in your heart.** Living the Mass doesn't end when we walk out of church, but it is then that our real work begins in the world. Consider how you might live out the Mass in one activity over the week. Who can you show love to? What is one thing we can work on this week as a family?

Pray: The Mass

Instead of rushing through the various prayers, enter the Mass and intentionally focus your heart and mind. On days when you cannot go to Mass, pray a spiritual communion such as this prayer from St. Alphonsus Liguori (1696–1787):

> My Jesus, I believe that you are present in the most Blessed Sacrament.
> I love you above all things and I desire to receive you into my soul.
> Since I cannot now receive you sacramentally, come at least spiritually
> into my heart. I embrace you as if you were already there and unite
> myself wholly to you.
> Amen.

Recommended Resources

For you: Living the Mass: How One Hour a Week Can Change Your Life, by Dominic Grasso and Joe Paprocki, is ideal for the countless Catholics who attend Mass simply out of habit, for the many who haven't been to Mass in a while, or for anyone seeking to join the Catholic Church. *Living the Mass* compellingly demonstrates how the one hour spent at Mass on Sunday can truly transform the other 167 hours of the week.

For your children: See *From Mass to Mission: Understanding Mass and Its Significance for Our Christian Life for Children* by Joyce Donohue. *From Mass to Mission* may be used with children from third to sixth grade in the classroom and with parents. Filled with fun activities, illustrations, photographs, and simple explanations, this booklet explains the meaning of the Mass and will help children understand why going to Mass on Sunday is so important for our faith.

5

Livin' on a Prayer: Questions about Prayer

Let me tell you a story about Grandma Dot, or "Nana Dot," as her grandchildren called her. Nana Dot had a strong Catholic faith and went to Mass daily. She prayed the Divine Mercy chaplet at three in the afternoon and her rosary right before she fell asleep. It was the highlight of her year when her eldest daughter, Kristin, her son-in-law, Kyle, and her grandson, Michael, came to spend a week in Oklahoma. Kristin was no longer practicing her Catholic faith, which was something that Nana Dot took to prayer every single day. The first time the family came to visit, Nana Dot took Michael to her local Catholic church to show him the beautiful stained-glass windows and some of the unique architectural features of the church. Nana Dot told Michael to whisper when they went into church just in case anyone else was praying there.

"We don't want to disturb anyone," she reminded him. "This is God's house, and many folks go there to pray and have a little peace and quiet." Michael didn't say a word, especially because Nana Dot had promised him ice cream afterward. Once they got to church, Nana Dot took Michael's hand and walked to the same pew that she sat in every day. After she genuflected, Nana Dot sat down with Michael and started to point out some of her favorite windows and art pieces in the church. "But the greatest treasure of all is right up there," she said, gesturing toward the tabernacle. "Do you see that red light?" Michael nodded. "When you see that red light, that's a reminder to us that Jesus is right here; that's a very special light." They sat together companionably in the silence. *This is going pretty well*, Nana Dot thought to herself as she squeezed Michael's little hand affectionately.

But Michael was starting to get a bit fidgety. After a few more wiggles in his seat, he loudly exclaimed, "OK, Nana Dot, I'm ready for ice cream now even though that red light still hasn't turned green!" It was then that Nana Dot realized that Michael had no idea who Jesus was and somehow thought the red light was a sort of traffic signal to enter and leave church!

While this story might make us chuckle, it's also a sad one in that Nana Dot realized that her grandson was growing up in a different world, one in which the familiar language of church was foreign to her grandson. The rhythm of Nana Dot's life was defined by faith: what time she went to church, what happened when she saw her friends, her charitable work through the Ladies' Rosary Society on Wednesday evenings, and their church social outings such as their bus trips and picnics. Michael was experiencing church as an unfamiliar place, like a stranger in a foreign land. Only one generation separated Nana Dot and Michael, but it felt as wide as a chasm. So, Nana Dot (with her daughter's permission) began to teach Michael about God, and they prayed every night together. "These were the happiest moments for me," Nana Dot shares. We may have similar moments with our family when we realize that faith is no longer taken for granted but one choice among many.

Parents, grandparents, and other important adults can build bridges of trust with young people in effective ways. This can be important "seed planting," especially with younger children, but even older children can be surprisingly open to religious experiences mediated through trusted adults. While it is the home environment that provides the greatest fertile ground for religious belief and practices, experiences with loved ones like Nana Dot can also open a child's eyes to God's presence, especially in prayer.

What is prayer?

—Alex, age 5

Prayer is when we talk to God to say thank you, to ask for help, to give God praise, or to share our concerns or feelings with God. To put it more simply, prayer is how we speak to God, heart to heart.

Relationships are built with time and trust. Helping your child to grow in trust of who God is and what he wants for your child's life is a life-long journey that is grounded in prayer. For our children to grow in their faith, they need to see us live out our faith first, and one of the best ways that we can do this is to live a life grounded in prayer. The *Catechism of the Catholic Church* tells us that "prayer and Christian life are insepara-ble" (*CCC#*2745) and that "prayer is a vital necessity" (*CCC#*2744).

Prayer is the sharing of our heart with God as we also listen to what he wants us to hear as well. God knows us better than anyone else as his beloved children and wants to be in close communication with us. As God's children, we are his most precious gift, and prayer is our gift back to God as we grow in our relationship with him. You can use formal prayers like the Our Father or Hail Mary, or you can just talk to God from your heart. As parents, we have a special and important role to play in helping our children come to know and love God.

How can I pray with my spouse?

—Wendy and Daniel, parents of one

Surprisingly, praying together can be difficult for couples, as Jane and Josh shared with me. "While I was on retreat, I heard that couples who pray together tend to have stronger marriages than those who don't, so I went home excited to share the news with my husband, Josh," she said. Lying in bed that night, Jane turned to Josh and said, "Honey, after what I heard this weekend, I would like us to pray together."

"Um, well, I've already said my prayers," Josh replied.

"No, no, I don't mean to pray silently." Jane said. "I want us to pray out loud together right now."

Jane and Josh lay in awkward silence for a few moments, and, thinking that her husband was composing himself to pronounce a prayer, she was surprised when he said quite loudly, "Well, I'm ready. You go first!"

"No, you go first," Jane said.

And back and forth it went like this for a few moments until Josh said, "I don't know what to say. I don't know what to do. Do we hold hands? Why is this so hard?" Both started to laugh at the absurdity of the situation!

This story crystallizes what many Catholics feel when they are asked to pray aloud with another. In general, Catholics haven't been taught to pray aloud with others in such a personal and intimate way, and at first, it can be an uncomfortable experience. This isn't a particularly Catholic problem but a part of our culture: increasingly, we do not talk about faith publicly because we are afraid of offending someone. Uplifting someone spontaneously in prayer is not something Catholics are taught to do, but that is also changing as more and more Catholics realize the importance of praying with others. It can feel jarring to verbalize our innermost prayers with another person, because we might have intensified feelings of vulnerability or inadequacy about the language we use. When we pray with someone, we speak heart to heart and allow others to be the voice of God to us. We expose who we are to God the Father, who sees each of us as we really are and yet loves us all the more. We fear that we don't have the "right" words or that we sound silly. This doesn't always make for an easy experience, but it is one that is rich, deep, and quite profound. Each time we pray with someone, we invite Jesus Christ to be present to us and to each other. This is humbling, and humility lays the foundation for prayer.

A simple formula for prayer helped Jane and Josh become more comfortable praying together. In our home, we call it the "whoops, wow, please, thank you" prayer.

Whoops: Reflect upon the moments of your day that were difficult, trying, or stressful. What moment from your day is weighing on you? Where did you make some mistakes? Where did you fail in your walk as a Christian? Confess that moment and express your sorrow for this "whoops" behavior. Ask God to help heal this situation so that you can be a more Christlike person and do better tomorrow.

Wow: As you look back on your day or week, identify those moments that were positive and joyful. Where were you at your best? Where did you feel the strength and power of God most fully? Express your praise and awe of the Lord and the wonderful world he has created.

Please: Is there a situation in your life that you are asking for increased prayer and help with? Name that situation and with sincerity, petition the Lord to take a hold of this situation and transform it. Be specific here and be honest.

Thank you: Take time to reflect upon and be grateful for all the blessings in your life. Thank God for each of these blessings and thank God for those around you who bring you daily reminders of his love. Say each name with a heart full of gratitude and love.

You can end your prayer with the Our Father, the Hail Mary, or another prayer of your choosing. You can even make one up, a prayer of your own heart! You can do this form of prayer as a couple or with your children or grandchildren, and you can hold hands, or incorporate silence or a Scripture reading as part of the experience also. You can do it with one person or around the table as a family. Make it a part of your day or your week. But my biggest piece of advice is that, no matter how you do it, actually *do* it. In all the years I have been asked to pray for someone, nobody has said no when I asked if I could pray with them in the moment. From these prayer experiences have come some of the most powerful moments of my life. Don't be afraid! Step out and give it a try.

How can I teach my children to pray?
—Christine and Alex, parents of four

One of the best ways that we can teach our children to pray is to model what it means to be a prayerful person. Children become comfortable with prayer if they see you praying. Children will come to see prayer as a natural and normal part of Catholic life if they see prayer interwoven throughout their day.

This means that we can pray *for* our children, pray *over* our children, and pray *with* our children. Let's go through the first two in more detail, and we'll save the third point for another section.

First, we can pray *for* our children. It sounds very basic, but we can sometimes forget that we can pray for our children by intentionally including them in our own prayers. For example, if you incorporate nighttime prayer as a couple into your bedtime routine, lift up your children in prayer and talk to God about your worries, concerns, hopes, and dreams for each child. We can entrust our children to our favorite saints and their intercession. We can call upon our own guardian angel and our children's guardian angels to protect them and keep them safe.

We can also pray for our children's vocation. A vocation is how God calls us to live and serve in the world. For some people, it will be through marriage; for others, it will be religious life and priesthood. Everyone has a vocation. My friend Eileen and her husband, Dave, have for years prayed for the future spouse for each of their three sons: "That whoever that God intends for our sons, that she is kept safe and knows how much that she will be loved in our family" is their prayer.

Second, we can pray *over* our children. Praying over our children can be as simple as incorporating prayer into our nighttime routine, or praying when we leave the house, take a trip, or gather for a meal. Like many parents of newborns, Joe and Emma would check on their sleeping son many times when they put him down to rest. They realized that this time could also be given to God, even the times when their child was sleeping. "We would tiptoe into Jeremiah's room to make sure he was okay because he could be croupy at night sometimes. While we were there together, we would extend our hands over him and pray silently for a few moments for his safety and health," Joe explains. This simple practice is a great example of praying over our children, even when they aren't aware of it. "Hovering in prayer" as Joe and Emma did is a simple technique to pray over our children.

Parent to Parent

Question: How can I incorporate some simple traditions into our regular routine as a family?

—Dominique, mother of five

Answer: Like most families, we would buy new shoes for the start of the school year. This was an important transition time for us because it always marked the end of a carefree summer back into the routine of school days. We realized that this time could become prayerful if we figured out how to ritualize it, so we came up with what we called the "blessing of the shoes." On the night before school started, we set out all the new shoes in our kitchen. We then took some holy water and blessed the shoes and our children's feet. We traced the sign of the cross on the soles of their feet and repeated a simple prayer such as "May God guide your steps in this new school year." With younger children who struggled to put on their shoes, we made the sign of the cross every time we put on or took off their shoes as a reminder that our steps should lead to God. It's funny because as the kids got older, we assumed that they would want to jettison this tradition, but they always reminded us to do it before the first night of school. Perhaps because they knew that they needed it more? Or the worries that they carried seemed bigger as they got older? Who knows? But this simple practice became a family tradition that has now been passed down to our grandchildren.

—*Tom and Ellen, parents of six, grandparents of three*

How do I get comfortable praying with others and also with my children?

—*Jamie, single father of two*

Jamie isn't the only parent to struggle with this. Keeping joy at the center of her life is something that Jessie and her 6-year-old son Andrew do together. Every night they pray. "We call it talking to Jesus," she says. "We begin with a traditional prayer (like the Hail Mary) and then we talk to Jesus using JOY—*J*, thank Jesus for a blessing; *O*, pray for others; and *Y*, ask for something for yourself." I then bless Andrew with holy water before he goes to sleep and say the same thing my mom did: "May Our Lady watch over you, protect you, and guard you as you sleep."

However you choose to pray with your children, a good rule is to pray "little and often," as my mother used to say. Regularity and consistency speak volumes rather than a long, drawn-out prayer done infrequently.

The Scriptures are clear—Jesus tells us to pray with others. The disciples asked Jesus to teach them to pray so that they could deepen their love for Christ and for one another. Many times, as Catholics we struggle to verbalize our prayers with one another, even with our own children. Pope Francis reminds us that "it is essential that children actually see that, for their parents, prayer is something truly important. Hence moments of family prayer and acts of devotion can be more powerful for evangelization than any catechism class or sermon" (*Amoris laetitia*, no. 288).

So, imagine that you are out and about and run into a friend you haven't seen in some time. After some conversation you notice that your friend seems worried and anxious. They open up to you about a situation in their life and ask for your prayers. The typical response from most people is "Of course I will pray for you," and then both of you move along with the rest of your day.

Instead of praying for that person and their situation later, however, why not pray for and with your friend in the moment? When you notice your children are anxious or upset, pray with them right at that moment! If you have a child with a major exam coming up, who struggles with test taking or test anxiety, sit down with your child and pray together for peace and for a good outcome for the test. Bringing prayer directly into the situation that your child faces builds trust and confidence among us and with God. This is known as share prayer, and the "Take It Home" section of this chapter contains a helpful overview of how you might pray this way with your children.

Does God answer prayers?
—*Kayla, age 7*

God always answers prayers, but in his own way and time. Even when we don't get the answer we want, with time and patience we learn that God does answer our prayers. We must remember that no is also an answer; so is silence. God might say, "Not yet" because it is not the right time, or yes, depending on the situation. The answer might not look like what we expect because God is God and we are not! This can be hard to explain to a child who is fervently praying for a sick loved one who then passes away. It can be tempting to offer platitudes such as "God only takes the best," but it is far more compassionate to acknowledge that we don't know why things happen like this, even when we pray. But we still pray and talk to God. Praying is important and we must be faithful, even in hard times.

What if I can't hear God anymore? Does God stop answering prayers?
—*Jeanelle, age 22*

Robert, a dear friend of mine, shared his sadness at God's apparent silence during a very trying time in his life. "I don't know if I can hear the voice of God anymore," he said. "I feel that I've been walking a lonely road for so long now and even though I set aside time to pray, I don't hear God speaking to me anymore. I feel lonely and abandoned," he tearfully shared.

When we are faced with moments of despair, doubt, and anxiety, we can wonder if God is silent in the face of our prayers and our tears. We may exclaim like the psalmists: "But I cry to you for help, Lord; in the morning, my prayer comes before you" and "Why, Lord, do you reject me and hide your face from me?" (Ps. 88: 13–14). Through our heartache, we wonder why the Lord seems to be silent in the face of our pain and why we cannot feel his comfort and love.

While on some level we know that God is love and that he loves each of us, when we do not hear him speaking to us, we begin to doubt and question ourselves and our relationship with God. We find this silence frustrating and painful. So, what can we do? Here are four suggestions.

Listen deeply. In the book of Kings, Elijah was told to stand at Mount Horeb to wait for the Lord to pass by. A great wind blew, followed by a mighty earthquake and a great fire. Elijah looked for God in the great wind, the earthquake, and the fire. But the Lord was not in any of them. Lastly, there was vast silence. As Elijah stood in the silence, the voice whispered, "What are you doing here Elijah?" (1 Kings 19:11–13). There is a great lesson for us in this. Listen not to ask for or to respond to but just listen. Listen at a deep level. Listen for the whisper of the Lord and dwell in that silence. God will speak, in his own time.

Let God be God. God is Lord of all, Lord of all the Earth, of all the chatter, and, yes, Lord of all silence! Remember that God is still present in the silence, and allowing this aspect of God's silence to wash over us may be a learning moment. Let God be God in his silence.

Keep talking. Through the silence, maintain a balance between silence and talking to God. Even when it feels hard, *especially* on days when it is hard, sincerely tell God that you trust him and ask him to heal any unbelief that you have in your heart. Let God speak to you through the Scriptures and draw comfort from his word. Reach out and tell someone that you are struggling with God's silence.

Know that God loves you. Every trial that we go through is an opportunity for us to grow closer to Christ, to grow deeper in faith, and to grow closer to others. Know that even in the silence, God is with you and loves you. Recognize anyone the Lord sends into your life to show you love.

One of the silver linings of God's silence is to highlight for us just how completely and utterly dependent we are on him. When Robert told me how difficult God's silence was for him, I reminded him of how beautiful his desire is for God to be present in his life. The world may tell us that we should avoid silence at all costs, but there is true value in the silence, even if we cannot see it at the time. Seeds grow in the silence and darkness of the earth. They are not buried in darkness; rather, they are planted to grow into the light, and so are we. Even though we cannot always see it, the seed of silence will bloom in love, and our prayer will bloom in God's time. We can also ask for help as we pray, and it is here that the Blessed Mother has an important part to play.

Do Catholics pray to Mary?

—José, age 13

José asked this question because he has a few friends who told him that Catholics do this, but it says in the Bible that we are only supposed to pray to God. "What's up with that?" José is asking.

The short answer is no, Catholics do not pray "to" Mary. We do not worship Mary or the saints in heaven. We pray to God, but we do ask for Mary's help in our prayers. This help is called *intercession.* Catholics worship God, but we do ask for Mary's help and the help of all the saints in heaven as we live our Catholic faith. Similar to asking someone to pray for us, we do the same with Mary. Her prayers are powerful because we know that Jesus loves her and listens to her.

Parent to Parent

Question: How do I help my children understand that God doesn't always act immediately when they pray?

—Nikita and Andres, parents of five

Answer: My daughter Elsie would always pray for a horse when she was a child. And I always told her that God would answer her prayers but that we might not get a horse. She didn't like that answer. But when my wife and I separated, Elsie and I moved to the country and, sure enough, next door to us, there was a horse ranch! God had answered her prayers but definitely not in the way any of us expected. Years later, when her mother and I reconciled, we all lived next to the horses, and Elsie told me that her prayers had come true. I think God knew exactly what he was doing, even when we couldn't see it. I wouldn't have wanted it any other way.

—Gary, father of one

Take It Home

Key Takeaways

- Prayer is the sharing of our heart with God as we listen to what he wants us to hear.
- We can pray for people, over people, and with people.
- Jesus models for us a life of prayer.
- Intercessory prayer connects us more deeply to the suffering of the other while at the same time encourages the Lord to take hold of our lives and our particular situations. We can "share prayer" with others as a simple way to acknowledge God's power and presence in our lives.
- Catholics do not pray "to" Mary but instead ask her to pray "for" us.

Reflect and Journal

As you go through the following list of common Catholic prayer practices, take an inventory of the ones that are a part of your life and the lives of your family. Which practices would you call the "staples"? Which ones do you not currently practice? Which ones could you add?

Habits of Prayer	Regularly Part of My Life	Infrequently Part of My Life	Practices I Would Like to Try
Morning prayer			
Mealtime prayer			
Daily Scripture reading			
Lectio divina			
Adoration			
Daily Mass			
Contemplative prayer			
The *Spiritual Exercises*			
Examination of conscience			
Corporal works of mercy			
Spiritual works of mercy			
Liturgy of the Hours			
Novenas			

Practice: "Share Prayer"

You have a friend who asks for prayer. Rather than waiting until later to pray in private, ask, "Would it be OK if I pray with you?" If your friend says no, just move on. If your friend says yes, you can follow the template below or improvise as the Holy Spirit moves you. You can use this prayer form in your family as well:

- Call on God in the following ways: God, Lord, Father, Jesus, Holy Spirit, Heavenly Father, Loving Creator, and so on.
- Thank God for the person you are praying with and ask for God's blessing: "Thank you for my friend, your son or daughter of Christ. Please bless my friend and uplift them at this time."
- Then ask God for what the person needs—for example: "We ask you to help Ann as she struggles with a health concern."
- Express gratitude for all that God is doing: "Thank you, Lord Jesus, for revealing yourself to us" or "Thank you for your blessings on this family."
- Finish the prayer with a doxology: "We ask this through Christ our Lord" or "We ask this in Jesus' name."

Pray: The Our Father

Pray slowly and meditate upon the words of the Our Father.

Recommended Resources

For you: Sacred Space: The Prayer Book, published by Loyola Press, will inspire you to a richer spiritual experience throughout the liturgical year and invite you to develop a closer relationship with God.

For your children: Loyola Kids Book of Everyday Prayers, by Catherine Odell and Margaret Savitskas, is an attractively presented book. Divided into nine chapters, it offers prayers from the traditional to all seasons and occasions.

6

What's the Closest Planet to Heaven? Questions about Heaven, Hell, and All in Between

You might remember I started off this book with the question from my son Sean: "What's the closest planet to heaven?" Have you figured out your own answer yet? Well, now is the time. Since we have covered some basic information and questions in the past few chapters, it's time to move on to more challenging and sensitive topics, including heaven, hell, and purgatory.

These issues are often the most difficult to address because they undergird sensitive scenarios in our lives. When my mother passed away some years ago, my son asked me a lot of questions about whether we would see Nanny again and whether she went right to heaven. At a time when our family was grieving, I realized that my answers in the moment weren't always the best answers, and so it was helpful to revisit the conversation at a later date. That's something we should remember as parents: if we are stumped in the moment, it can be helpful to have an initial conversation and then revisit it later. Opening with something direct like, "Remember that conversation we had about Nanny going to heaven a couple of weeks ago? Well, I've been thinking about it and want to talk to you about it again since this is such an important topic" can be a helpful way to open up dialogue. You will need to have multiple conversations about the questions in these areas, and depending on your child's age, you can go into more or less detail as you deem appropriate. With that being said, let's get started on some of the obvious questions that children might ask and move to those that stretch us a little more throughout the chapter.

Is there life after death?
—Jayden, age 14

Yes! As Catholics, we believe in an afterlife, which we refer to as *eternal life*. Our belief in an afterlife or eternal life is based on the resurrection of Jesus Christ. While our bodies are buried, we believe that our soul goes to God for judgment. This is known as *particular judgment*, when the Lord judges our life worthy of joining him in heaven or if we choose separation from God for all eternity, which is hell. The period of waiting for this judgment is called *purgatory*. The concept of purgatory can open up a can of worms, so let's treat questions about purgatory in a few moments.

Where is heaven?
—Carter, age 6

"If heaven is all about sitting around and praying all day," little 5-year-old Ted said to his parents, "I definitely don't want to go there! It sounds so boring."

The word *heaven*, when used in the Bible, can mean a few different things: the place where God and the angels live, a space beyond what we experience in this world, and even a reference to the sky. Generally, though, when the Bible speaks of heaven, it speaks of a place or a state of being with God. It can be tempting to think of heaven as "up there," but it's important to help children understand that heaven is a perfect state of being with God.

The timing of when we talk about heaven is just as important as the way we talk about heaven, as a grief support counselor once pointed out to me. "If we always link heaven with loss and death, then it's no wonder that children may have mixed feelings about the whole concept," Devon reminded me.

Heaven is a state of complete unity with God and the complete fulfillment of all our human longings. The *Catechism* defines it as follows: "Heaven is the ultimate end and fulfillment of the deepest human longings, the state of supreme, definitive happiness" (*CCC* #1024).

The *Baltimore Catechism* was the official book of Catholic teachings for use in the United States up until the universal *Catechism of the Catholic Church* for the entire world was published in 1992. The *Baltimore Catechism* contained 421 questions and answers about the Catholic faith and included a very succinct definition of why God made us, which includes a simple reference to heaven. Question: Why did God make us? Answer: God made me to know him, to love him, and to serve him in this world, and to be happy with him forever in heaven.

How do you get to heaven?
—*Adriana, age 14*

"Heaven is God's home, and all of our lives are about preparing to be with God in his special home" is how Daisy answered this question when asked by her 5-year-old son.

This is a good start to a conversation about how we might get to heaven. In the Bible, Jesus addresses this question, indicating that it is by placing our trust in him and by following him that we get to heaven; he says, "I am the way, and the truth, and the life. No one comes to the Father except through me" (John 14:6). So, we follow Jesus and do what he asked us to do. It sounds simple, but we all know that living a Christian life is anything but! Keeping the commandments, loving God and one another, going to Mass, frequenting the sacraments, and taking care of those who are less fortunate than ourselves are all ways that we can live a Christian life and, with God's grace, be in heaven with him.

Does everyone get to go to heaven?

—James, age 7

This is another tricky question, but if we speak of heaven as a state of complete happiness, then why wouldn't children want to know if their family and friends are in heaven? A simple answer might be to tackle it by emphasizing that those who die in God's grace and who are heartily sorry for their sins and failings will be with God our Father in heaven. While we cannot definitively say that someone is in heaven or in hell, we have hope that God will show mercy upon his beloved children, especially those who want to be with him forever. In 1 Timothy 2:4, St. Paul says that God "desires everyone to be saved and to come to the knowledge of the truth," which means that God wants each of us, when it is our time, to be with him in heaven.

Do animals go to heaven?

—Emma, age 12

This is a hard one on multiple levels. But the answer is "maybe." Animals do have souls but not in the same way that humans do. Interestingly, the word *animal* comes from the Latin word *anima*, which means "soul." But since only humans, angels, and God have *eternal* souls, traditional Catholic theology teaches that animals do not have eternal souls. Because every creature on Earth "reflects in its own way a ray of God's infinite wisdom and goodness" (*CCC* #339), we have reason to hope that in the "new heaven and earth" that will be created at the end of time (Rev. 21:1; Isa. 65:17), animals will be present in heaven.

Here's how one parent, a mother of four, answered her children's questions when their dog Shadow passed away: "God blesses all creation and calls it good. We shared lots of love with Shadow and took care of her, and love comes from God, so yes, God loves Shadow and wants to pet her too, just like we did. And then we talked about the birth of Jesus, the stable, with all those animals surrounding Jesus. Animals were a part of the life of Jesus, Mary, Joseph, the Holy Family. There are animals in heaven, too, and Shadow will be there and will remember us when we get there too. She'll come a-running to greet us."

Do people who die become angels?
—Jonathan, age 14

You might be confused hearing statements like "heaven has gained another angel" or "he/she got their wings" when someone we love dies. But despite these well-meaning statements we will not become angels after we die. God created the angels, and one primary task of the angels is to minister to us human beings. God created us, too, as a different kind of being, made of physical elements but also given souls through God's own breath and spirit. Angels might take human form but are spiritual beings, different from us in creation and purpose. The Bible never indicates that we will change our created form to become angels.

What is a guardian angel?
—Hannah, age 6

Many of us know the prayer: "Angel of God my guardian dear, to whom God's love commits me here, ever this day be at my side, to light, to guard, to rule, to guide." But what exactly is a guardian angel? A guardian angel is the messenger of God's love who is sent as a guide, protector, and guardian for us to remind us of God's love and care. The word *angel* comes from the Greek word "messenger," and so angels are messengers of God's love. The existence of angels is a truth of our faith, and each of us has a guardian angel.

What will happen to my disability in heaven? Will I still have diabetes?
—Raven, age 8

My daughter Ava developed Lyme disease when she was four. Although she is much better today, this was undoubtedly a time punctuated by a lot of worry, prayer, and stress in our home. Her illness was on everyone's heart and mind. I remember her asking me, "Will I ever get better, Mama, and if I don't get better, will I have Lyme disease in heaven?" Questions about suffering and particularly the suffering of little children are among the hardest to answer.

But one way to explain this is to say that if heaven is a state of perfect being with God where there is no pain or sadness, then whatever burdens us or troubles us in life will be gone. So whatever disabilities or sicknesses were present on earth will be taken from us so that we can be perfectly at peace and fulfilled with God.

What will we do in heaven?
—John-Thomas, age 9

This is a similar question to the one I referenced earlier from Ted, who complained that heaven sounded terribly boring! To be fair to little Ted, he is not wrong; how we often speak about heaven can be quite cringey and insipid. My advice here is to tap into the *why* behind the *what*. I happen to know that the little boy John-Thomas who asked this question is very passionate about horses and horse riding. I would address his question by starting with horse riding and how God wants us to be completely happy and at peace with him in heaven. So, we will have fun, we will celebrate, we will praise God, and we will be filled with joy. Whatever we need to be completely happy we will have in heaven, and that includes horses! Most excitingly, we will also see the face of Jesus, as Revelation 22:4–5 tells us. We will have everything we ever want or need in heaven.

Will we have a body in heaven?

—*Katie, age 11*

Yes! In the Apostles' Creed we say the words that we believe in the "resurrection of the body," which means that we will have bodies in heaven. But they are "glorified bodies," far better than the ones we have now, since they will be completely free from sin, disease, and illness. For that we can be especially grateful!

In heaven will we recognize the friends and loved ones we knew on Earth?

—*Anna, age 16*

It is only natural to be concerned about those we love and whether we will see them again. When my mother passed away, I remember how comforting it was to know that one day I would see her face again and hear her voice. Our conversations over tea in the kitchen would not be over! So, yes, we will recognize our friends and loved ones in heaven. When someone dies and we have a funeral, the priest prays from what is called the Rite of Christian Burial the following words: "May we comfort one another with our faith, until we all meet in Christ and are with you and [the name of the one who has died] forever. Through Christ our Lord." This means that while we will not exactly look the same as we did on Earth, in heaven we will be able to see all those we long to see and be with.

Parent to Parent

Question: When my grandchildren ask me if what happens at Mass is real and true, what do I tell them?

—Pedro, father of eight, grandfather of six

Answer: As a family, we were watching a very popular children's movie together, when midway through the movie, a scene alluded to the death of one of the parents. My husband and I stopped the movie to talk with our children about what was happening, but I could tell that my youngest son, Sean, was troubled. "Mom, I don't want anyone from our family to die," he said with tears in his eyes. "Because, Mom, I'm the youngest and I don't want to be left alone. If everyone is older in the family, I will be the last one left," he said as he climbed onto my lap. That night, we talked and prayed together as a family, lifting up all our family members who had gone before us to eternal life, but the conversation did not seem to be settled, at least in Sean's mind.

A couple of days later as I was tucking him into bed, Sean sat right up as if he had just connected something in his mind and was having an "aha!" moment.

"Mom, Mom, is it true?" he said excitedly. "Is what true, Son?" I asked.

"You know how at Mass, Father says to us that if we eat this bread, we will live forever?" With an expectant expression on his small face, he held his chubby hands outstretched as if he were holding the Eucharist between them, just as he had seen our pastor do at Mass. "Mom, is that true?" he asked. "Because if that is true, we will never die, right, Mom?"

I felt my eyes filling with tears.

In the Gospel of John, we hear the words of Jesus to each of us: "I am the living bread that came down from heaven. Whoever eats of this bread will live forever; and the bread that I will give for the life of the world is my flesh" (6:51). This is what we as Catholics call the real presence. Just as Jesus is so present to us in the Eucharist, we have to ask ourselves if we are really present to him. Rather than being present to our worries, doubts, and fears, can we set those all aside and enter his sacred presence with the faith of a child?

We have made steady advancements and progress in the Western world in our mortality rates. People live longer today than ever before. And yet, the one gift that will truly give us the grace to live eternally is the gift of love and sacrifice made for each of us in the real presence of Christ in the Most Holy Eucharist.

"Is it true?" my son asked me with a sense of expectant hope. And I answered with every fiber of my being.

"Yes, son, it is true. He is true and we will live with him forever."

—*Wayne and Julianne, parents of three*

What is hell? Is it real?
—Johan, age 12

In a world that sometimes glorifies being a "badass," hell is often depicted as a cool place full of excitement, which is unfortunate. When it comes to the topic of hell, I often start with some simple information: just as heaven is not a place, neither is hell. There is no place or destination that we can point to that is hell. But heaven and hell are real, and it is important to be clear about this. Indeed, "the teaching of the Church affirms the existence of hell and its eternity" (*CCC* #1035). If hell is the opposite of heaven, which is complete unity with God, then hell is a state of having no connection with God at all. In that state, we experience only a void, a state of being in which we choose to be completely separate from God. It is an abyss in which we experience no love, no mercy, no hope, and no goodness.

Levi, father of four, indicates that the casualness with which we discuss hell in the culture bothers him. "I remember the first time that I heard the phrase 'Hell, no!' and it completely stopped me in my tracks," he says. "Although I wasn't quite sure what 'hell no' meant at first, I quickly learned that it was a way of emphasizing a point of disagreement on a particular matter. I'm no prude," Levi admits, "but when we bandy around 'hell no,' it reduces hell to something silly and trite, which it definitely isn't."

Levi makes a good point. It's important to be prudent and careful with this topic. In popular culture, the idea of hell has been reduced to rebelliousness, but it is far more serious. There are consequences for how we choose to live and act, and if heaven is a choice, then so is hell. An under- or overemphasis on hell can actually be harmful. Denying the existence of hell and portraying God only as a God of "fire and brimstone" are not only inaccurate but dangerous. When we talk with our children about hell, we need to be especially careful.

Is Hitler in hell?
—*Isaac, age 12*

As a former middle school theology teacher, if I had a dollar for every time one of my students asked this question, I would be a rich woman indeed! Many times my students would try to think of the most villainous characters from history or the present time to debate who would or would not end up in hell.

Let's start with something very important. God does not *want* anyone to go to hell (see *CCC* #1037). Not one person. We ought never to be complacent in thinking that we are going to automatically end up in heaven or in hell. Or that others are going to go there. We put ourselves in hell by our own actions.

The *Catechism* indicates that for people to go to hell, a "willful turning away from God (a mortal sin) is necessary, and persistence in it until the end" (*CCC* #1037). Although we cannot say for sure that people like Hitler are in hell, it is clear that there are people who choose to go there as a result of their own actions.

Can you be a good person and go to hell?
—*twins Amber and James, age 8*

If you asked a group of people what constitutes a "good person," you would likely find that their answers would be all over the place.

Each one of us will live out our faith differently, and that is a good thing. Doing our best to live our faith is always a good thing. We have to remember, though, that our faith is not all about what we do, although that's important. It is about our faith in Jesus Christ and our belief in his goodness, mercy, and love.

What is purgatory?
—Brielle, age 9

"My priest explained it this way. Purgatory is like the security checkpoint at the airport. You have your ticket, and you know that you're getting on the plane. But there are certain things you are not supposed to take on. So you empty your pockets and go through the metal detector. When you are ready, you board! Heaven is the final destination." This is the explanation from Cynthia, grandmother of fourteen.

In the Bible we are told that nothing unclean will enter heaven; as Matthew 5:8 reminds us, "Blessed are the pure in heart, for they will see God." Purgatory is getting your heart cleaned up so you can meet God. It is not "spiritual jail." The good news about purgatory is that if we make it there, we are assured of going to heaven.

Sam, who teaches middle school, often uses the analogy of an elevator to explain purgatory. "Purgatory is like an elevator on the way to the top floor (heaven). We know the end is heaven, but we are in the elevator and traveling until God indicates that we are ready to meet him." It is a matter of when, not if. Purgatory readies us to be in full union with God our Father.

I heard my grandmother talking about "limbo." What's that?
—Jason, age 17

Many people believed that children who died without being baptized went to a place called limbo to await their judgment. Limbo comes from the Latin word meaning "border" or "threshold." For many years limbo was a part of the church's common tradition, meaning that it was a part of the lived experience in parishes and mentioned in older catechisms. Many people believed that this was doctrinal teaching, which contributed to a lot of misunderstanding and pain on the topic.

However, it is important to note that limbo has never been an official part of the Church's doctrinal tradition and therefore we are not obliged to believe in it. It is not a part of the *Catechism of the Catholic Church* today.

Will I see the child I miscarried someday?

—Shanisha, mother of four

The best answer to this question comes from a very painful story shared by Tara and Derrick, parents of three, two earthly children and one heavenly: "I was looking forward to seeing our family to tell them the good news: we were expecting our second child. But when I awoke the morning of our trip, I knew that something was seriously wrong. At the hospital, the doctors carried out an ultrasound and found that our baby had a serious heart defect. 'You will most likely lose this baby, Tara,' our doctor said. 'There's nothing we can do or give you at this point; all we can tell you is to rest. I'm so sorry.'"

"That afternoon I lost my baby," said Tara. "There was no body, there was no funeral, but the grief was overwhelming." During this time, my husband, Derrick, asked our pastor, "Father, we don't know why this happened, but I have to know—is our child in heaven?"

"Father had tears in his eyes as he responded: 'Your child is with God in heaven, of that I'm certain. God is a loving father, and while we do not know why you suffered this loss, God knows why, and one day you will see your child again.'"

"Father then invited us to the 'infant life and loss' ceremony that took place a few times during the year, remembering all those who had lost a child. Seeing my child's name in print was incredibly powerful; our child had a name, what happened was real, and our suffering had meaning! To this day, the loss of our second child reduces me to tears, but I take great comfort in knowing that I will get to hold my child."

In this painful story lies the truth at the heart of our faith: our God is a merciful one who loves us greatly, and we have the hope of everlasting life with him. I myself lost a preborn baby, which was a heartbreaking experience, and so I have talked about this issue a few times with my own children. When we go to the grave of our son Christopher Joseph, we often have very deep conversations afterward as a family. I have answered this question for my own children by emphasizing that children are especially precious to God, and he knows what is in our hearts. God is a loving God and wants each of us to choose to be with him. When a baby dies before baptism, we trust that this child will be with God in heaven. This has been such a comfort to me and my children.

The reality of topics can be emotional ones for us and our children, but as difficult as it is to explain these concepts, it is important that we do so.

Giving children a strong foundation in these areas will mean that they are more likely to understand the church's position as one of love rather than judgment. This is especially important when it comes to the moral teachings of the church, the topic of the next chapter.

Take It Home

Key Takeaways

- God wants us to be in union with him.
- God does not will anyone to hell.
- Hell is a void, or the absence of God's love.
- Heaven is our ultimate home, a state of supreme happiness with God, and the complete fulfillment of all desires.
- Purgatory readies us to be in full union with God our Father.

One good tactic to encourage children in their call to holiness is to build the virtues that lie within them. The virtues help us do what is good and avoid what is not good for us. The *Catechism* defines virtue as "habitual and firm disposition to do good" (1833). The Catholic Church lists seven virtues, with four being primary or "cardinal" virtues. The term "cardinal" comes from the Latin word *cardo*, which means "hinge"; so much of our behavior hinges on their foundation. These cardinal virtues are prudence, justice, fortitude, and temperance. There are three other theological virtues: faith, hope, and charity or love.

Reflect and Journal

As you think about the concepts of heaven and hell, what is a new insight that the stories in this chapter have given you? As a Catholic, are you living in such a way that acknowledges the reality of heaven and hell? What fears do you have as you think about the topics in this chapter?

A Reflection on the Virtues

Name of Virtue	What It Means	Further Reading	Reflect
Prudence	This is the chief or "driver virtue" that guides justice, fortitude, and temperance. Prudence helps us do the right thing and attain the good in every situation.	CCC #1806	
Justice	Justice is giving to God and our neighbor what is right and just. This virtue helps us to respect God and all people.	CCC #1807	
Fortitude	Fortitude helps us remain courageous and constant when we face struggles.	CCC #1808	
Temperance	Temperance helps us maintain self-control and balance in daily life.	CCC #1809	
Faith	Faith is a gift that grants us the willingness to commit to God, do our best to serve him, and be a witness to the Gospel.	CCC #1812–1814	
Hope	Hope inspires in us a desire for abundant life now and everlasting life with Jesus.	CCC #1817–1821	
Charity or Love	This virtue encourages a deeper love of God and of neighbor. The fruits of charity are joy, peace, and mercy.	CCC #1822–1829	

Practice: For Those in Purgatory

An older but often forgotten prayer practice is to pray for those in purgatory. This prayer from St. Gertrude the Great is a powerful prayer:

> Eternal Father, I offer you the Most Precious Blood of your Divine Son, Jesus, in union with the masses said throughout the world today, for all the holy souls in purgatory, for sinners everywhere, for sinners in the universal church, those in my own home and within my family. Amen.

Consider incorporating this prayer into your family routine.

Pray: For Those Who Have No One

Once, as we were praying as a family, I asked the children if there was anyone we should pray for. After we named family and friends, my son Ian asked that we pray for "those who have no one to pray for them." This is a simple practice but reminds us that there are many throughout the world who have no one to pray for them.

Recommended Resources

For you: Watch the movie *Heaven Is for Real* (rated PG), a 2014 film written and directed by Randall Wallace and cowritten by Christopher Parker. It is based on Pastor Todd Burpo and Lynn Vincent's book of the same name. *Heaven Is for Real* recounts the true story of a small-town father who must find the courage and conviction to share his son's extraordinary, life-changing experience with the world.

For your children: Read *My Path to Heaven: A Young Person's Guide to the Faith*, by Geoffrey Bliss. *My Path to Heaven* is a "retreat in a book" that helps Catholic children, ages 9–12, ponder the truths of the faith and calls them to live lives of holiness in accordance with those truths. Based on the traditional St. Ignatius retreat and adapted for children, this clear, simple, and thoughtful presentation of the Catholic faith is invaluable for parents seeking to form their children in holiness.

7

Birds, Bees, Flowers, Trees: Difficult Moral Questions

Today, we face a world that is less receptive to organized religion. We live in what has been called a secular age. What does this mean? When it comes to more difficult moral issues, many believe that the Catholic Church should offer no public commentary on the poor, on the misuse of resources, on systems that oppress others, on economic advancement, on science, and the list goes on. This of course goes against the core of the Gospel message! Faith is certainly personal, but it is not meant to be kept private. We should not allow society, politics, or culture to set the agenda for how we teach our children about faith. But we need to search for entry points into the lives of our children, and that includes our culture. St. Ignatius of Loyola spoke of this as "entering through their door but leaving through your own." As parents, our task is to identify these doorways and introduce through them the light of our faith in Jesus Christ.

Jesus' Approach to Difficult Questions

As the source of love and truth himself, Jesus spoke love and truth into the heart of every person he encountered. He spoke to the relevant cultural issues of the day, whether it was religious difference, slavery, or the freedoms of men and women. He spoke about marriage, sex, divorce, violence, and money. He spoke about the political system, about brokenness, heartache, and apathy. He spoke to people in private and in large public crowds. Jesus teaches us that there is a right time to discuss more sensitive issues, and here are two principles he demonstrated.

Some discussions are better held in private. Something to consider is that when Jesus encountered difficult situations, the conversations he had often happened in private, such as with the "woman at the well" who was living with a man who was not her husband, and with Nicodemus, who came to Jesus at night. Having conversations in private with your children helps them feel safe and loved, especially when it concerns the more sensitive topics of how we ought to live. Our parental approach needs to be modeled less on a lecturer or professor (a sage on the stage) and more on Jesus' approach, which includes listening, teaching, loving, and keeping the dialogue open (a guide-on-the-side approach).

Our children need to be confident that we hear them. Jesus teaches us that people are most open to new insights only after they have been heard, respected, and honored. For older children or young adults, this may mean that when they say something that is not quite correct, instead of correcting them right away or shutting them down (especially when others are present), we listen to understand, not just to respond. We can correct after we have listened well so that we understand the context behind the question.

Remember, too, that faith-based conversations in sensitive areas of sexuality and identity are likely going to run countercultural to the dominant cultural narrative that bombards your child on a regular basis. Listening deeply for the reason behind the question, and possibly the pain, will be critical to keeping the conversation going.

While we must talk about the consequences of our actions with our children, we also need to talk about God's love and mercy, and the Bible gives us some great guidance in how to do this.

Steady Eddie and Reckless Rick

In the Gospel of Luke 15:11–32, we meet two very different sons with two very different ways of approaching life, love, and forgiveness. We meet one son who strives to do everything right, saves his money, and stays home with his father—a classic "steady Eddie," if you will. But he harbors resentment toward his younger brother, whom he judges to be selfish and whom he condemns for his foolish behavior. This younger brother seems to be a reckless squanderer who leaves home and lives a life of indulgence, selfishness, and waste, spending his father's inheritance. Let's call him a "reckless Rick." A story of two brothers, one selfish and reckless, the other selfless on the surface but underneath resentful and grudging. But in the middle of the story stands the father, God our Father. When the younger brother returns home—spent, depleted, and truly sorry—his father's arms are outstretched in love. But the older brother, instead of being overjoyed to see his long-lost brother, chastises his father for his generosity and forgiveness, saying, "All these years I have been working like a slave for you, and I have never disobeyed your command; yet you never gave me even a young goat so that I might celebrate with my friends. But when this son of yours came back, who has devoured your property with prostitutes, you killed the fatted calf for him!" (Luke 15:29–30). The Father reminds the older son that this is a time to celebrate "and rejoice, because this brother of yours was dead and has come to life; he was lost and has been found" (Luke 15:32).

Rather than dwelling on the failings of the two sons, it is important to look to the heart of the story, to the heart of the father, who extends goodness and mercy to both children but especially to the younger son, reckless Rick. God never closes his arms to us. We close ourselves off to his love. We have all been one son or the other at various times, and it is far too easy to dwell on the sins of others and overlook our own failings. Whatever life throws at us, we have to remind our children that even when things get messy, we will be there for them with outstretched arms, like God the Father.

In matters of morality, the Church's teachings are rooted in the premise that there is a natural law established by God. The *Catechism of the Catholic Church* states that "the natural law, the Creator's very good work, provides the solid foundation on which man can build the structure of moral rules to guide his choices" (*CCC* #1959). Natural law is a body of unchanging universal moral principles that provide the basis for all human conduct. This "natural law is written and engraved on the soul" of each person (*CCC* #1954). Natural law gives us the universal basis for a whole host of issues, including murder, kidnapping, abuse, and same-sex attraction. This natural law is "present in the heart" (*CCC* #1956) of every person since God created us and helps us to follow God more closely. Natural laws are for the good of all of us. For example, a universally acknowledged principle is "Thou shall not kill." Murder is a violation of natural law. Natural laws are not rooted in bigotry or hatred but in compassion, truth, and love because they are rooted in who God is. They may be difficult to accept, especially for teenagers, but there are good reasons for them. As we approach difficult questions, particularly in the area of morality, here are a few important insights that parents shared:

- **Pray.** Before any difficult conversations with your child, pray. Even if you are caught off guard and are asked a question on the spot, it's always good to pray with your child in the moment to acknowledge tough questions and that we need to ask for God's help.

- **Reflect.** Some of our responses as parents are very much shaped by how our own parents talked to us about sex. Some parents handled these conversations with grace, others by avoiding them or passing along inaccurate information. Yet if we approach these conversations with obvious discomfort and awkwardness, this communicates something important to our children—that sexuality is awkward and uncomfortable and that we aren't open to a conversation about it. Reflect on your experience and intentionally decide how you want to shape these conversations.

- **Research.** Discover what the Church teaches on topics and why those beliefs are important for us today. Your personal belief and witness are hugely important, but clarity of information is going to be just as important in dealing with more difficult questions.

- **Discover.** Find out what your child already knows when they broach a sticky issue by asking questions like, "What have you heard?" and "What do you think about that?"

- **Answer.** Give simple, age-appropriate answers. Don't feel the need to divulge huge amounts of information unless your child continues to follow up with more and more questions.

- **Search.** Search your own heart with respect to the Church's teachings and practices. You may unwittingly be passing along your own insecurities and doubts about certain areas of the Church's teachings.

- **Same page.** Make sure that you and your spouse are on the same page with respect to how to handle tricky issues. This is especially important in families where parents do not live in the same home. Taking the time to check in on these important conversations can lead to less turmoil down the road.

- **Model.** Be a witness of love and charity for all of God's people, even for those who may have different beliefs from your own.

- **Follow up.** These are not one-time conversations. Follow up often with your child and check in on where your child is.

Where do babies come from?
—*George, age 6*

With very young children, it is important to remember that when they ask about where babies come from, they are not asking about sex per se but about the biology behind it. They may be genuinely curious about a "baby bump." You can respond with something simple such as "Babies come from God, and they are inside Mommy's tummy until they are ready to be born" and see where that leads.

This answer may then trigger the next question, which may be along the lines of "But how do they get out of your tummy?" Consider responding, "When it is the right time, the doctor helps the baby come out," and leave it at that. Some parents do choose to disclose more information, especially related to biology, and use the correct anatomical terms, but that is a matter of knowing your child and their readiness for such concepts. If you do choose to go that route, make sure that you and your husband are on the same page with respect to terminology and how to address various facets of the biology.

How is a baby made?
—*Marina, age 8*

This question is a bit more advanced than the previous question. With slightly older children, it is fine to share something simple: "A special part of Mommy and Daddy come together to make a baby." This may or may not lead to more questions, including what specific parts come together. The key here is to stay open to the discussion and to model good listening skills so that children cultivate a healthy understanding of God's plan for their lives, including their sexuality.

Can people who aren't married have babies?

—Jeremiah, age 10

Here's how Patricia addressed this question with her son: "My sister Kathy has four children with two different fathers but has never been married. Lately, Jeremiah has been asking questions about Kathy and her boyfriend and is pretty confused about marriage. We sat down and discussed the situation more than one time. I reminded Jeremiah that while it's true that people can have babies without being married, that we as Catholics believe that it is important to be married so that God can bless our families in a special way since there are special blessings that come with being married and having babies later. While I want Jeremiah to understand the possibility of having babies outside of marriage and I don't want to unfairly judge my sister, I also want him to understand that marriage confers special graces on a relationship."

As Patricia acknowledges, there is a balance between unfairly judging someone's situation and also clearly sharing what your own family and indeed the Church believes.

Sex before marriage; what's the big deal?

—Miles, age 14

During the teenage years, dating and relationships take center stage as young people explore all aspects of their identity, including their sexuality. They push against all kinds of ideas and boundaries and begin to experiment with new attitudes, behaviors, and ideas.

This specific question represents the countercultural narrative of "try before you buy" when navigating relationships, dating, and sex. In our culture, sex is often seen as a means to an end rather than a gift to be embraced. Sex outside marriage and "hooking up" are considered no big deal. But they are. There are repercussions for all our decisions but especially because sexuality affects us profoundly.

One of the ways we communicate how we feel about someone is through physical intimacy. This is a facet of who we are and is a good thing. Tell your children that physical intimacy is beautiful. Part of opening a healthy conversation with your children about sex is to affirm that sex is beautiful in the proper context. So many people are scarred by conversations with their parents who told them that sex is bad, when of course it is not when it happens in the appropriate time, place, and stage of life.

You can then move to the next stage of the conversation: because we as Catholics see sexual activity as a great gift, it is important to wait until marriage to have sex. The gift of our sexuality is not something to be traded away but rather protected. Sexual intimacy is not just a physical act; it also involves all aspects of our emotions, intellect, and spirit. Young people are still maturing in these areas, and even if they feel a strong sexual pull in a relationship, they are likely not ready emotionally for the impact a sexual relationship will have on their whole life. You can explain this as a natural reason that sex should happen within a stable (married) relationship. Chastity is a real sacrifice—it's important to acknowledge this—but a healthy and whole relationship in marriage is worth waiting for.

Sexual activity is not a means to an end; it finds its fullest expression in marriage. One of the ultimate purposes of marriage is to have children, and it is best to wait until marriage for lots of good reasons that you can share if your child is open to hearing more about them.

What does "having sex" mean?
—*Lilly, age 12*

This is a great question for modeling Jesus' methodology of asking questions. You could ask any of the following:

- What have you heard about what having sex means?
- When have you heard people talking about having sex?
- Is having sex something that you are curious about? Why?

This will naturally open dialogue. For younger children, a simple answer such as "Sex is when a man and a woman come together to make a baby" may be helpful.

Why does the Catholic Church hate gay people?
—Alyssa, age 16

Of all the questions we have tackled so far, this is one of the hardest to answer. Young people ask this question because the Catholic Church and Catholics in general are often viewed as intolerant and out of touch with the world around them when it comes to this issue. This is unfortunate because the Church's teachings in relation to sexuality have often been woefully misconstrued. And what doesn't help are Catholics, especially those in positions of leadership, who have acted shamefully and not honored Jesus' commandment: "Just as I have loved you, love one another" (John 13:34).

When the Church truly follows Jesus and its own teachings, it does not express hate toward anybody, especially those who are suffering or going through any kind of difficulty, including those who struggle with their sexuality. Many of those who experience same-sex attraction have experienced prejudice, discrimination, and violence. The *Catechism* states that persons who have an inclination to have sex with others of their same sex "must be accepted with respect, compassion, and sensitivity. Every sign of unjust discrimination in their regard should be avoided" (*CCC* #2358). Jesus wants all people to come to friendship with him, including those who experience same-sex attraction. As a Church, we can do much better to provide support and care to those who are struggling with same-sex attraction.

The Catholic Church teaches that sexual acts between people of the same sex are not morally acceptable. The Church's teachings are rooted in what is best for the human person, and the Church declares that sexual activity be reserved for those who are married and who are of the opposite sex. One of the purposes of marriage is to have children, and that is possible only between a man and a woman. God designed our world to work that way, and the Church cannot change what God has designed. We see this in the book of Genesis where "God created humankind in his image, in the image of God he created them; male and female he created them" (1:27).

But, just as it is not morally acceptable for anybody to engage in sexual acts outside of marriage, it not morally acceptable for those who experience same-sex attraction to engage in sexual acts outside of marriage.

Is there support in the Catholic Church for those who experience same-sex attraction?
—*Claire, age 12*

There is support for those who experience same-sex attraction. People are always our best resource in caring for other people. As such, our Catholic communities ought to be spaces of healing, support, and prayer for all people, but sadly, this is not always the case. There are some great organizations such as Eden Invitation helping to support young people. There is also a national organization approved by the Catholic Church called Courage International. This is an apostolate that offers pastoral support to men and women experiencing same-sex attractions who have chosen to live a chaste life. EnCourage is a ministry within Courage dedicated to the spiritual needs of parents, siblings, children, and other relatives and friends of persons who have same-sex attractions. Living a chaste life means that those who experience same-sex attraction will live out the virtue of chastity and refrain from sexual activity outside of the Sacrament of Marriage, which is reserved for marriage between a man and a woman. Many parishes and schools around the country have Courage chapters to help support families and individuals. If your school or parish does not have one, consider approaching the leadership to start one. Also, Catholic Charities offices throughout the country offer excellent counseling services to support youth, young adults, and adults.

Parent to Parent

Question: What do I do if one of my children tells me that they are experiencing same-sex attraction? How do I respond?

—*Kristin and Darius, parents of four*

Answer: Parents, push aside everything else—your own fear for their future, your own disappointment in them not having grandchildren, your fear of discrimination for them in housing or in the job market, or marital status from one state to another, or HIV/AIDS, or what the neighbors will think. Ask your child to tell you their story. You will learn to see with new eyes and a new heart. Tell them you'll need help with this and that you don't know it all but want to learn. And you love them. Plain and simple. If you have negative feelings, be sure your child doesn't hear you discussing them. This is critical. This may take a while to get to this fully accepting and loving point. The mom may come to being more understanding before the dad, or vice versa. (This can cause marital tension, big time.) Do *not ever* kick them out of your home. Homelessness and suicide rates are sky-high with our young people.

—*Michele, mom of four, grandmother of four*

What does the Church teach about gender fluidity or being transgender?
—Thomas, age 15

God wants each of us to be healthy—physically, emotionally, mentally, and spiritually. In other words, God wants us to be whole people. The Catholic Church's teaching on gender is connected to our biological sex and our spirituality and cannot be separated from it. The *Catechism* states that "by creating the human being man and woman, God gives personal dignity equally to the one and the other. Each of them, man and woman, should acknowledge and accept his sexual identity" (*CCC* #2393). As a result, the Catholic Church does not teach that a person's gender can be different from their biological sex or that their gender or sex can fall into a spectrum or be fluid.

How does a girl become a boy?
—Andrew, age 6

Andrew, who asked this question, has a cousin who identifies as transgender and sometimes is confused when looking at pictures of his cousin. Here's how Andrew's mom, Jessie, responded to this question:

"Sometimes people feel different on the inside than they look on the outside, so they want their insides and outsides to match. Even though God made them the way they are. Some people talk with a doctor to figure out why they feel that way. Some people go to a doctor to try and make their insides and outsides match. The most important thing is to love people no matter what and to try and help them love themselves the way God made them."

Why can't Catholics get divorced?
—Paul, age 13

Divorce is one of the most painful experiences that parents, and their children, can go through. When I met my husband, Wayne, he often talked about his parents' divorce and how it affected him for the rest of his life. He describes his parents' divorce as "a complete loss of home and family." Thirty years later, he still gets emotional talking about the day that he found out that his family would change forever. Divorce is a major life event. For some families, like my husband's, it is devastating. For other families, the divorce process can be freeing, providing a fresh start that might bring feelings of relief, hope, and peace again.

Let's start with a critical point: all of us are worthy of love. We are capable of giving and withholding love. When a couple gets married, they do so with the best of intentions to love and care for each other forever. Sometimes, though, relationships break down to the point of separation or divorce. Divorce is a legal separation that ends the marriage. Divorces are painful for everyone.

The Catholic Church understands that sometimes men and women enter relationships that break down, and it is better for both people to no longer be married. Catholics can get divorced because marriage is not just a church process but also a civil process that comes with legal rights and obligations. However, because Catholics believe that marriage is such a special gift from God, we also have a process called an *annulment* because marriage is not just a civil process but also a religious process. Vows are taken before God. An annulment is a process that examines whether, in the eyes of the church, there were issues that caused the marriage to be invalidated. An example of when an annulment would be granted is if one person was previously married but did not tell the new spouse, or if one person was engaged in a serious relationship with someone else during the time of their marriage.

Many children worry how an annulment affects them or if they are considered illegitimate or nullified. Rest assured, because an annulment deals only with what happened between spouses, the process does not change the relationship of the parents to the children. Neither God nor the Catholic Church views children of divorced parents any differently.

Why can't women be priests?
—*Avé, age 14*

Many young people are motivated by justice and fairness and can perceive the Church to be unfair in the issue of ordination. Young people look up to leaders and want to be leaders themselves. Ordination is often seen as the only path to leadership in the Catholic Church. It is important to listen for the issue of power or authority that your child is wrestling with. Priesthood is often conflated with power rather than service. Women can hold key positions of power, service, and leadership in the Church, just not as a priest. Talk with your children about how they see priests and what kinds of things that priests do. Emphasize that many of the things that they see priests doing are things all of us can and should do, such as visiting the sick, feeding the hungry and homeless, and making the world a more humane place.

When we pray the Apostles' Creed, which is a statement of our beliefs, we say that the Church is "one, holy and apostolic." The word *apostolic* means that the teachings of the Church go right back to the apostles. Although he counted women such as Mary Magdalene among his closest disciples, we see from the Scriptures that Jesus did not choose women to be among his twelve apostles. The Church cannot change its teaching on this issue because this teaching was given by God to us. Mary holds a special place in our Church as a woman, and women play an important role in the life of the Church. Indeed, the first person the resurrected Jesus appeared to was a woman, Mary Magdalene.

Why is the Church against contraception?
—*Jenna, age 17*

Contraception and having children go hand in hand. Children are a gift and a blessing. The Catholic Church allows a married couple through natural family planning to use their judgment in providing for their family. This is because natural family planning is open to life at all stages and does not require medications, devices, or surgery to regulate the natural process of conception. Artificial contraception such as the birth-control pill blocks or prevents a couple from conceiving a child and bringing new life into the world. Instead of allowing God to bless us naturally with life, we block God and his plan for our life.

Today the Church's teaching is finding new appreciation from those who are more health conscious. Many people who are conscious of the negative impact of contraception on the human body actually find Catholic teaching refreshing in its holistic approach!

Natural family planning is consistent with God's plan because it enables a husband and wife to work with the body rather than against it. Fertility is viewed as a gift and a reality to live, not a problem to be solved, and our openness to fertility respects God's design for married love.

Does the Church look down on IVF? Why?

—*Carlie, age 15*

Artificial interference in our efforts to have a child is something that the Church is rightly concerned about. Human life begins at the moment of conception. This is not just the Catholic Church's teaching but science also supports this claim. Modern genetics has established that a human being's DNA is created when the sperm fertilizes the egg and creates an embryo. At this moment of conception, a unique human person is created. The process of in vitro fertilization brings together the sperm and the egg in a laboratory but does not fully respect human life. For example, for in vitro fertilization to be effective, multiple human embryos are created, and the overwhelming majority are destroyed in the process. This by-product of in vitro fertilization is a willful destruction of innocent human lives, and it is not often well known and represented.

What's the Church's teaching on surrogacy?
—*Ivan, age 15*

Surrogacy involves a woman agreeing to carry a baby for someone else. After the baby is born, the surrogate mother gives custody to the intended parents. There are many ethical issues when it comes to surrogacy. Because in vitro fertilization is involved, multiple embryos are selected and rejected in the process, and this destroys life. Through scientific interference, surrogacy also bypasses God's intended plan for us to marry and have children.

Abortion—why is the Church against it?
—*André, age 17*

The Catholic Church values all life from the moment of conception to natural death, and abortion prematurely ends the life of an innocent child, no matter how early or how far along the pregnancy is. This has been a part of the Church's earliest traditions regarding life and death when it confronted pagan cultures that often engaged in the practices of human sacrifice and abortion. For example, in pre-Christian cultures, ritualistic human sacrifices were common, such as the "bog people" recovered in Europe. The bog people are the naturally preserved corpses of humans and some animals recovered from peat bogs. The bodies have been found in Denmark, Germany, the Netherlands, the United Kingdom, and Ireland. Many of the bodies such as the famous Tollund Man were victims of human sacrifice. It was also not an uncommon practice in some early cultures to leave "deformed" infants out in the elements to die—or to allow girl babies to die. The earliest widely used documents of Christian teaching and practice after the New Testament in the first and second centuries, called the *Didache* (or "Teaching of the Twelve Apostles"), and the

Letter of Barnabas condemned both practices, as did early regional and particular Church councils.

The *Catechism of the Catholic Church* states that "since the first century the church has affirmed the moral evil of every procured abortion. This teaching has not changed and remains unchangeable. Direct abortion, that is to say, abortion willed either as an end or a means, is gravely contrary to the moral law" (*CCC #2271*).

Depending on the age of the child, you might want to also address the issue of whether the baby is a "sentient being" who deserves our protection as a person and under the law. There are many who claim that preborn children or children in the womb do not deserve respect or should not be treated as persons because they are so early in their development. However, all life is sacred, and people should be treated with dignity and respect regardless of factors such as age, condition, location, or lack of mental or physical abilities. That some are more worthy of rights than others denies the very idea of inherent human rights, which come from God and should be respected and protected universally.

For any woman who has had an abortion, the Catholic Church offers love, mercy, and forgiveness through Project Rachel. Project Rachel is a diocese-based network of specially trained priests, religious, counselors, and laypersons who provide a team response of care for those suffering in the aftermath of abortion. This ministry provides an integrated network of services, including pastoral counseling, support groups, retreats, and referrals to licensed mental health professionals and makes the Sacrament of Reconciliation available to those touched by the pain of abortion.

Can Catholics get a tattoo?
—Samantha, age 13

We believe that our bodies have dignity and value because they are created in the image of God. As such, it is important to take care of our bodies as a temple of the Holy Spirit who dwells within us. Many Catholics draw on the passage from Leviticus 19:28 to point out that people should not get tattoos: "You shall not . . . tattoo any marks upon you. I am the Lord." Generally, the Catholic Church upholds only Old Testament laws that are timeless moral laws; many laws from Leviticus were written to address a specific issue at the time. For example, the Leviticus passage in this case prohibits tattooing as a practice that honors false gods. So, Catholics can certainly get tattoos and, as with all practices of body modification, should make sure that it does not dishonor God. Even though throughout this book wisdom from the *Catechism* has been shared, there is a very helpful addition to the *Catechism* called the *Compendium to the Catechism* that gives very clear directions regarding practices such as this.

Well, friends, this chapter has been a difficult one to write. I hope it gives you some clear information that you can use to talk to your children, grandchildren, and students in a way that is healthy and faithful to the Church's teachings. For the next chapter, we'll stick with some of these more challenging areas as we delve into questions that relate to sin and suffering.

Take It Home

Key Takeaways

- The Catholic Church bases much of its teachings regarding morality on natural law.
- Natural law is a body of unchanging moral principles that are the basis for all human conduct.
- The Catholic Church does not "hate" anyone, including those who have gotten divorced, are struggling with their sexuality, or have committed grave sin.
- Marriage is a gift from God.
- Our bodies are temples of the Holy Spirit. We should avoid anything that gives offense to God.

Reflect and Journal

Nowadays Christianity of the past is often criticized as having been opposed to the body; and it is quite true that tendencies of this sort have always existed. Yet the contemporary way of exalting the body is deceptive. Eros, reduced to pure "sex," has become a commodity, a mere "thing" to be bought and sold, or rather, man himself becomes a commodity.
—Pope Benedict XVI, *On Christian Love*

What personal experiences in the area of sexual morality can you share with your children when appropriate? Which questions are the most difficult for you to address? How can you help your children develop a strong moral foundation? In the chart that follows on the next page are topics and scriptural readings that can help you and your children expand the conversation and respond to questions and uncertainties that arise.

Biblical Discussion Starters about Relationships and Sexuality

Topic	Reading	Our Thoughts
Our sexuality is a gift from God.	Read Genesis 2:22–24	
Our sexuality is good.	Read Genesis 1 26:27	
We express our sexuality as men and women.	Read Genesis 1:27	
Marriage is defined as between a man and a woman.	Read Mark 10:69	
Jesus teaches us that condemnation and judgment about sexuality are not appropriate.	Read John 8:1–11	
All are called to faithfulness in our relationships.	Read Deuteronomy 5:18	
All are called to practice chastity.	Read Ephesians 5:3	
God is merciful when we make mistakes.	Read Matthew 5:7	
God is a God of Love who wants the best for us.	Read John 3:16–17	

Practice: Set Boundaries

Talk about healthy and unhealthy boundaries with your children. Setting and maintaining boundaries is an important part of human development. We can set boundaries when it comes to our mental, physical, emotional, spiritual, and sexual health, including boundaries for our children. For example, family members or friends will give and expect in return hugs, kisses, and snuggles from our children. However, some children are naturally less affectionate than other children, and their boundaries need to be respected. Practice talking about healthy and unhealthy boundaries as a family.

Pray: The Peace Prayer

The Peace Prayer of St. Francis covers a great deal of spiritual ground in helping us to be at peace in the midst of difficult conversations:

Lord, make me an instrument of Your peace. Where there is hatred, let me sow love; where there is injury, pardon; where there is doubt, faith; where there is despair, hope; where there is darkness, light; where there is sadness, joy.

O, Divine Master, grant that I may not so much seek to be consoled as to console; to be understood as to understand; to be loved as to love; For it is in giving that we receive; it is in pardoning that we are pardoned; it is in dying that we are born again to eternal life.
Amen.

Recommended Resources

For you: Learn more about the apostolates Courage International and EnCourage International. Both council men and women in the areas of same-sex attraction. Visit www.couragerc.org to learn more.

For your children: Watch the movie *Bella* together. Rated PG-13, *Bella* is an inspiring movie about a loving and compassionate man who falls in love with a troubled and lonely woman. Together they discover the gift of love and life. Note that abortion comes up as one of the options the main character considers when she finds out that she's pregnant. Ultimately, she decides to keep her baby after an encounter with someone who changes her mind.

8

Sin, Suffering, and Salvation

"There's no guilt like Catholic guilt and no Catholic guilt like Irish Catholic guilt." I heard this many times growing up in Ireland. Let's be honest, who hasn't heard a joke or two about "good old Catholic guilt"? Although less common today, many people associate Catholicism with guilt and shame, as this story reveals.

A few years ago, I had a phone call from Marcella, who was carrying tremendous heartache because of her experiences as a teenager. When Marcella found herself pregnant, her parents kicked her out of the family's home and sent her away to live with her grandparents. Unfortunately, her grandfather told her that because she had a baby outside of marriage, she was no longer welcome in "God's house" (meaning the Catholic Church) and that it was likely that she would go to hell. What a terrible response to the birth of a child!

This lovely woman carried the pain of this experience for years and believed that, because of her guilt and shame, God had rejected her. One day, thirty years later, she was driving and saw a sign inviting people to come back to the practice of their Catholic faith. Bravely, she made a phone call to one of our offices at the diocese, and someone connected her with me. After briefly talking over the phone, I invited her to come and meet face-to-face, and so she came to see me. During that visit she poured out her heart to me. Through her tears she told me how much she had been missing God. I reached out to hold her hand and told her that she had been treated shamefully and that God loved her and did not want her to suffer. Although at first afraid, she asked to see a priest, and I was able to connect her with one of the most compassionate priests that I know. She came back to my office a month later, and I noticed right away the change in her face and in her very bearing. She looked as if a huge weight had been lifted from her shoulders, and she appeared to be at peace. I told her that it was so good to see her happy, and she responded, "The weight of my shame and guilt at being abandoned by so many people has begun to heal." She was attending Mass for the first time in thirty years. "I wept when I received communion," she shared, "after being away for so many years."

There are many Marcellas in our midst today, people who have left the Catholic Church after an unkind and unchristian encounter with a family member, a parishioner, a parish staff member, or a priest. These moments can have a profoundly negative impact on someone's life. In our conversations with our children, they may unfortunately hear stories such as this or even the more mundane stories of "unchristian Christians" who have, by their witness, pushed people away from practicing their faith. It is important as a parent to be able to navigate these moments and not dodge the harder conversations about our own faults and failings as a people and as a church. As we all know, guilt is not always a good motivator to practice our faith because it can often lead to feelings of shame. Shame and guilt, while connected, are not the same. Guilt is often an emotion that arises because of a behavior or activity. Shame is connected to your deepest identity and focuses not just on the behavior or event but on your *self*. Guilt says, "What happened was bad," whereas shame says, "*You* are bad."

As you engage in difficult conversations with your children, pay attention to any feelings of guilt or shame that arise in them and talk about them directly. Don't allow conversations to fester. While sometimes it is good to take a step back and allow time for questions "to breathe," when there are hard conversations, staying connected is the key. Now let's turn to some tough questions around sin, suffering, and salvation beginning with some general questions and then transitioning to more specific questions from children.

What is evil?
—*Jamal, age 15*

Using the word *what* here is helpful because evil is not a thing, an entity, or a being. That may seem confusing, but it is more apt to describe evil in terms of what it is not: it is not love, not good, not true, not beautiful, and therefore not of God. For young children, describing evil as the opposite of goodness and love would be accurate.

For older children, you might want to go into more detail, and our faith provides some helpful insights from the saints here. Evil is the opposite of God. Just a quick note on Catholic philosophy here: Catholicism has been influenced by the lives of the saints, and one of the foremost thinkers about Catholicism was St. Thomas Aquinas, whose theories and ideas are very much part and parcel of our faith today. One of his enduring insights concerns what evil is and what it is not. St. Thomas Aquinas describes evil as a *privation*, or, to put it in simpler terms, as a lack or a void. So a lack of goodness, of love, or of mercy can be described as a form of evil. To make this concrete, when we tell a lie, the evil that is present is a void or a lack of truth.

Why does God allow evil to exist?
—*Cai, age 16*

The phrasing of this question is important. God allows evil to exist but does not create it. Because evil is a lack or void, it is not a thing to be created. When talking to our children about evil, we should also distinguish between two kinds of evil: moral and physical. Moral evil includes murder and theft, for example. Physical evil, however, describes famine (lack of food), illness (lack of health), natural disasters, and death. God loves us and so created us with free will, which is the capacity to embrace God or to reject him and choose something else. Relationship with God is at the heart of our faith, and God would never force us to love him, because love, by its nature, does not force anyone. We have many choices in life, and the consequences of our own choices often lead to moral evil. When it comes to physical evils such as natural disasters, God does not cause them but permits them to happen for some greater good that we are not always aware of.

Why do bad things happen to good people?
—*Enola, age 17*

Similar to the previous question, this one brings the reality of evil down to a more concrete situation. At the heart of this question is the issue of suffering and why good people suffer. Suffering is a natural part of life, and yet most of us, rather than embrace it, run from it or drown in it. This is only natural, because suffering can be intensely painful, leaving us feeling exposed and vulnerable. It is hard to see as a gift something that is painful. When we think of gifts, we naturally think about what makes us happy or content rather than something that stretches us, pushes us, or brings us to our knees. Nobody is spared from suffering. This tells us that it is a natural part of the universal condition, and there must be good reasons we go through times of suffering, which are often accompanied by lots of tears.

Suffering can always bring growth, even when we cannot see it. During times of suffering, we go through the process of conversion, and our attitude and behavior are refined and purified. With time and God's grace, we come to understand that a particular suffering, while not pleasant, was a gift, for it allowed something new to emerge.

Conversion takes place, and resistance and grieving give way to acceptance and new life. Through these intense periods of suffering, God is continually transforming us to be more compassionate, more hopeful, more merciful, and more loving—all attributes of Christ.

Why does God allow us to die?

—Gino, age 10

Back we go to the beginning! In the book of Genesis, we learn that God created Adam and Eve to be in relationship with him and to take care of all that he had created. He pronounces all of creation to be good, but when Adam and Eve are created, "God saw everything that he had made, and indeed, it was very good" (Gen. 1:31). This is the first time we hear God use the phrase "very good," which tells us something about his plan for us. God's original plan for humanity was complete communion and unity with him, a state of perfection, a state of heaven! As created by him, we are "very good."

As such, death was not a part of God's original plan for us. But how did death enter the Garden of Eden? It entered through what is called the Fall, or the doctrine of original sin. Sin entered the world when Adam and Eve disobeyed God of their own free will and fell from grace and from perfection. As a result, sin and death entered our lives when Adam and Eve rebelled against God, preferring to be gods unto themselves. The effects of their sin have contaminated all their offspring, and so every marriage and family, and the first place we see this is in Adam and Eve's own family. Cain killed his brother Abel (see chapter 4 of Genesis). Do we see what has happened because of this sin? Marriage and family life, the centerpiece of God's work, became fragmented and broken. But Jesus Christ came to save us from the permanent destruction of sin, and so we are redeemed and saved by his love.

Why did God allow my friend to die of cancer?

—*Tessa, age 9*

My heart aches when I hear questions like this from young people. The pain behind these questions cuts to the core of whether God is truly what he says he is: a God of mercy and love in the face of suffering, pain, and loss.

When someone we love dies, it can be hard to think that God let it happen. We may feel angry or upset with God. We imagine that God is unkind and unfeeling. But we must remember that God does not cause our death, even if he allows or permits it. While we don't always know why some people die sooner than others, we do know that God understands our pain because his own son was put to death. It can be tempting to think that because we are angry with God he doesn't care about our pain, but we learn in the Bible that he is patient with us: "The Lord is merciful and gracious, slow to anger and abounding in steadfast love" (Ps. 103:8) and he is "rich in mercy" (Eph. 2:4).

Why is suicide wrong?

—*Jayden, age 13*

The pain of suicide touches us all deeply and we must have compassion for those who have died this way or those who have attempted to end their life by suicide. Attempted suicide is when people hurt themselves with the intention of ending their own life. When someone dies in this way, we say that they have died by suicide. For children between the ages of 10 and 14, suicide is the second leading cause of death, which is a frightening statistic. Young people are swimming in a world of pain and increased mental health issues.

Pope Francis reminds us that "when it comes to suicide, we cannot look away. Instead, we must look upon others with the face of love as Jesus looked at all whom he met" (*Evangelii gaudium*, no. 75). "Love is our best means of helping people who are suffering to see the value in their own life. Our lives are not our own as the *Catechism* tells us: our lives belong to God. We are stewards, not owners, of the life God has entrusted to us. It is not ours to dispose of" (*CCC* #2280). As such, suicide is gravely wrong, but God has compassion for all who are suffering and in pain. "The Church prays for persons who have taken their own lives" (*CCC* #2283), and so should we. We also need to be vigilant in understanding suicide and how to identify suicidal ideation in ourselves and others. Mental health and first-aid training can be an important tool to help us understand the reality and impact of suicide today.

If God made us like him and he is perfect, then why do I need glasses?
—Ian, age 12

My son Ian asked me this question one night. He has had glasses since kindergarten and has really struggled with the desire to be rid of them. I explained to Ian that as God's children, each of us is made to reflect him. This means that each person is like God in some way. But we are also individuals who are unique in God's eyes. Some people have stronger legs than others for running fast. Some have stronger voices for singing. Some have stronger eyesight. Our bodies all have some sort of imperfection. These imperfections teach us to see differently—in the case of someone who struggles with their eyesight, physical sight is only one dimension of sight. God also blesses us with spiritual sight so that we can see God in ourselves and all around us. I explained to Ian that he is so conscious of his sight, which is teaching him to look with the eyes of compassion upon the world.

Why doesn't God intervene during a war when people are suffering?

—Michael, age 15

War, unfortunately, is as old as humanity itself. Where you find envy, greed, and power, you will also find war, strife, and division. But it is important to remember that God does not cause wars, even when people argue about the best way to worship him, as in the case of the Catholic and Protestant conflict in Northern Ireland. A wise friend of mine reminded me some years ago that the word *ego* stands for "edging God out." At the heart of war is ego—the ego of those who covet what does not belong to them, the ego of those who think they are superior to others, the ego of those who play God with the lives of others.

Trying to edge God out of our lives is something that human beings have done since the dawn of time, and the Bible is replete with clear examples of this. In the book of Genesis, we see the egotism of Adam and Eve, who lied and tried to edge God out of the Garden of Eden. In the book of Exodus, we see the egotism of the Israelites, who made a golden calf for themselves to worship. In the New Testament we meet the Pharisees, who edge God out through an overzealous focus on the law that leads them to rigidity and legalism. Behind and in the middle of all disunity and discord is the evil one. The devil is the king of ego and the usurper of peace. It is he who profits most from war, division, and hatred. But we know from Jesus' example on the cross that ego and power will never have the last word, as our faith teaches us. God does not intervene in a war but permits it to happen because God does not force people to act a certain way, and so people cause war through their greed and lust for power. However, God will take any situation and bring good from it, even if the situation was not one God desired for us.

Does God cause disasters like hurricanes and tornadoes?

—*Robin, age 12*

Hurricanes and tornadoes fall under the realm of physical evils such as natural disasters caused by natural phenomena such as inclement weather and storms. God does not cause them directly but allows them to happen so that good may come from them.

My dad never goes to church— will he get to heaven?

—*twins Kevin and Anabell, age 14*

The best answer to this question was given by Pope Francis. At a question-and-answer session at St. Paul of the Cross parish in Rome on April 15, 2018, a little boy named Emanuele whispered his question into the pope's ear because he was so overcome with emotion that he could not express it. The pope repeated the question for the audience, indicating that the boy's father was a nonbeliever who had passed away but had all four of his children baptized. Emanuele told Pope Francis that his father was a good man and had asked him, "Is my dad in heaven?"

This is what the pope said to those who were present:

> How beautiful to hear a son say of his father, "He was good." And what a beautiful witness of a son who inherited the strength of his father, who had the courage to cry in front of all of us. If that man was able to make his children like that, then it's true, he was a good man. He was a good man.
>
> That man did not have the gift of faith, he wasn't a believer, but he had his children baptized. He had a good heart.

Then Pope Francis began to answer Emanuele's question by asking the children present to consider what kind of heart God our Father has: "What do you think? A father's heart. God has a dad's heart. And with a dad who was not a believer, but who baptized his children and gave them that bravura, do you think God would be able to leave him far from himself?"

"Does God abandon his children?" the pope asked. "Does God abandon his children when they are good?"

The children all shouted back loudly, "No!"

"There, Emanuele, that is the answer, God surely was proud of your father, because it is easier as a believer to baptize your children than to baptize them when you are not a believer. Surely this pleased God very much."

This was a great answer by Pope Francis for it allowed the children to consider the attributes of God and how God wants all who are good and who desire to be with him to get to heaven. When it comes to those who do not believe in God, God allows them to freely choose him in death. We have hope that we will see our loved ones once again because they will be with God.

Are ghosts real?

—Asher, age 7

As Catholics we believe in the Holy Spirit. As we discussed earlier, the Holy Spirit was called the Holy Ghost, which comes from the Old English word for spirit: *gast*. But when we talk about ghosts, most people are thinking about supernatural or paranormal beings. There is no official Catholic doctrinal teaching on ghosts; however, the Catholic Church does affirm that sometimes the spirits of those who have died, such as the saints, do appear to others. St. Maria Goretti appeared to her murderer, Alessandro Serenelli, in prison. St. Padre Pio also indicated that he had been visited by those who had died. So, on the topic of ghosts, the Catholic Church does not say much, but on the topic of spirits, it has quite a lot to say.

Are the saints spirits?

—Jonah, age 14

The saints were all real people just like you and me. They lived in our world and tried to do their best to know, love, and serve God and pursue holiness. We honor saints with celebrations on their feast days—for example, St. Brigid on February 1 and St. Anselm on April 21. The saints are not spirits, but they live with God in heaven. We can ask them to pray for us. Asking someone to pray for us is called *intercession*. The saints are great intercessors for us.

What does the Church teach about magic or things like Ouija boards?

—Gary, age 16

We believe in a world created by God in which there are things that we cannot see—supernatural realities that are no less real than what we can see and touch with our own hands. For that reason, any attempt to control the future, to practice witchcraft, sorcery, or magic, is strictly forbidden by the church and gravely detrimental to our spiritual health. By trying to know the future, we put ourselves in place of God, which is a violation of the First Commandment, which teaches us: "I am the Lord your God . . . you shall have no other Gods before me" (Ex. 20:2–6). Trying to communicate with those who have died (besides asking our loved ones to pray for us), such as using Ouija boards or participating in séances, is forbidden by the Church. This is what the *Catechism* says: "All practices of magic or sorcery, by which one attempts to tame occult powers, so as to place them at one's service and have a supernatural power over others—even if this were for the sake of restoring their health—are gravely contrary to the virtue of religion" (*CCC* #2117). Now, this does not mean that we can't talk to our loved ones who have passed away, but asking them to intervene in our lives or using them to obtain power or pass on knowledge is forbidden.

What is a demon?
—Elizabeth, age 10

In the Bible we meet many characters who are afflicted by demons. One of Jesus' early miracles was curing a person afflicted with demons who was disrupting a synagogue teaching in Capernaum. Another name for a demon is "evil spirit." In the Bible we also hear that demons are fallen angels who sided with Satan instead of God. In the Gospel of Luke, we hear that an evil spirit entered Judas and caused Judas to betray Jesus. The Catholic Church does not deny the existence of evil spirits and has a special ritual that casts them out, which is called an exorcism.

What is an exorcism?
—Ken, age 19

There are instances when a person needs protection against the devil and evil spirits. In the Bible, we read that Jesus cast out evil spirits and demonic activity (see Mark 1:34, 39; Luke 4:35; Matt. 17:18). An exorcism is a special type of prayer that the church uses against the power of the devil and evil spirits.

Sometimes, the Church carries out an exorcism. Exorcisms are divided into two kinds. The first kind includes simple or minor forms of exorcism, such as for those who are preparing for baptism, in the Rite of Christian Initiation of Adults or the Rite of Baptism for Children. During these rites we invoke God's help and protection against any powers of darkness.

The second kind of exorcism is the one most popularly portrayed in the media. It is considered a "major exorcism," which is a rite that can be performed only by a bishop or by a priest. In the case of a priest who wants to carry out a major exorcism, he can do so only with the express permission of the bishop. A major exorcism is directed "at the expulsion of demons or to the liberation [of a person] from demonic possession" (*CCC* #1673).

It's important that children understand that God's power is greater than any evil spirit—and that demons are not allowed to simply enter people or terrorize us, which is the impression a person might get from watching certain horror movies. Many cases of demonic activity begin with a person intentionally dabbling in the occult (such as using Ouija boards) or overtly choosing evil. Evil practices are a gateway for demonic activity and should be avoided. We need to acknowledge the power of evil but not fear it and ask God to protect and guide us.

Will the world end?
—*Jason, age 16*

The very last book of the Bible is the book of Revelation, which speaks symbolically about the end of time. It reveals that the struggles we face in this life will come to an end through Jesus, who will return in glory. This is often referred to as the "second coming of Christ." While many people have tried to figure out the exact date and time of the end of the world, this is beyond our comprehension and understanding. God alone knows when our time will end and when Jesus will come again. Jesus was also asked this question and responded, "Keep awake therefore, for you do not know on what day your Lord is coming" (Matt. 24:42). For all of us, the world will one day end with our own death. But what we consider death is the beginning of eternal life, as St. Thérèse of Lisieux reminded us when she said, "I am not dying, I am entering life." The Church does not teach a definitive end to the world that will take place at a particular time but instead tells us to be ready by loving and serving God so that he may come and make "all things new" (Rev. 21:5).

Some of the more difficult questions in this chapter center on evil, death, and demonic activity. We must address questions about these topics in a way that does not provoke deeper curiosity in evil and the occult. The word *occult* comes from Latin *occultare* and means "to conceal." Usually what is being obtained from such practices is secret information coming from outside forces that are not always benign. We must be matter of fact about the topic but very clear about the effects of dabbling in the occult, which can open us up to demonic activity in ways we might not be fully aware of. This is why it is important to immerse your family in the smells, bells, and practices of our Catholic faith. Going to Mass, receiving the sacraments, and wearing sacramentals that "are sacred signs which bear a resemblance to the sacraments" help us to continue to turn our heart and mind to God.

Take It Home

Key Takeaways

- Evil is a lack or a void. God does not create or cause evil.
- It is God who remains the sovereign master of life. We are stewards, not owners, of the life God has entrusted to us.
- Saints are not spirits; they live forever in harmony with God in heaven.
- The Catholic Church does not deny the existence of evil spirits and has a special ritual that casts them out. This rite is performed by a priest and is called an exorcism.

Reflect and Journal

Consider your life. Have there been any practices that you didn't realize were harmful, such as Ouija boards or tarot cards, that you were exposed to or participated in? Have you spoken to a priest about this or sought out the Sacrament of Reconciliation? How can you protect your family from being exposed to occult practices such as sorcery, tarot cards, and even television shows that depict such activities as normal?

Sometimes our children struggle to identify with saints who seem so far away from their own experience of life. Pick one of the saints from the chart below, explore their story, and learn from their witness.

Ten Mighty Saints

For when you need:	Name of Saint	How Can I Relate?
Courage	St. Joan of Arc (1412–1431)	
Determination	St. Elizabeth of Hungary (1207–1231)	
Resilience	St. Pedro Calungsod (1654–1672)	
Patience	St. John Berchmans (1599–1621)	
Inspiration	St. Clelia Barbieri (1847–1870)	
Mental Health	St. Dymphna (7th Century)	
Faith	St. José Luis Sánchez del Río (1913–1928)	
Perseverance	St. Kizito (1872–1886)	
Gentleness	St. Gemma Galgani (1878–1903)	

Practice: Celebrating All Souls' Day

Helping our children understand that death is a natural part of our Catholic life can be an important part of developing an appreciation for life. The feast of All Souls' Day is a day of holiness when we remember the loving-kindness of our God toward those who have died and grieve for those we have lost. The Eucharistic Prayer for various needs (#4) in the Roman Missal encourages us to "remember also those who have died in the peace of your Christ and all the dead, whose faith you alone have known. To all of us, your children, grant, O merciful Father, that we may enter into a heavenly inheritance with the blessed Virgin Mary, Mother of God, with blessed Joseph, her Spouse, and with your Apostles and Saints in your kingdom."

You could have your own celebration at home by taking out pictures of loved ones who have passed away and displaying them in a special place in the home. At a special time, gather your family around these pictures. Play some soothing music and light a candle. Everyone can share memories of the person or persons you are honoring. You can conclude with a simple prayer such as the one below.

Pray: For All Souls

Prayer Leader: May the love of God and the peace of
the Lord Jesus Christ bless and console us and gently wipe every
tear from our eyes.
In the name of the Father, and of the Son, and of the Holy Spirit.
All respond: Amen.
Prayer Leader: Eternal rest grant unto them, O Lord,
All respond: And let perpetual light shine upon them.
Prayer Leader: May their souls and all the souls of the
faithful departed, through the mercy of God,
All respond: Rest in peace.
Prayer Leader: Go in the peace of Christ.
All respond: Thanks be to God.
Amen.

Recommended Resources

For you: An excerpt from the book *Parenting a Grieving Child: Helping Children Find Faith, Hope, and Healing after the Loss of a Loved One*, by Mary DeTurris Poust:

Don't get into comparisons. One death is not worse than or better than another. Even the death of a goldfish can be a huge loss for a child.

Be compassionate and allow the child to feel sad or angry.

Don't be fooled by outward behavior. Children sometimes appear unaffected by loss, but in reality their grief will come out at some point. You can help it along by being available to a child in grief—to listen, to play, to cry, to pray.

Ask simple questions or make simple statements that help a child articulate his own feelings:

- "It sure is quiet around the house without Spot's barking. I miss him."

- "How are you feeling today? Do you want to go for a walk with me?"

- "This was Grandma's favorite [song, season, food, sweater, etc.].
  Remember when [recall a specific event]?"
- "Would you like to keep this [book, doll, necklace, etc.] as a
  reminder of your sister?"

For your children: Let your child see your own grief. Don't be afraid
to be sad together. Say a favorite prayer together or make something
up as you go along. You can use the reflection "Healing the Hurt" as
a guide:

Losing someone we love
is like losing a part of ourselves.
We feel an ache inside,
an emptiness that can't be filled.

Dear God,
give us the wisdom and grace
to recognize that ache
in the children we love and serve.
Help us say the right words,
do the right thing, as we
guide them on the path toward
healing and wholeness.
Amen.

Faith and Science:
Big Bang or Big Bust?

Young people are naturally curious about the world. They want to learn, and they have an insatiable appetite for asking questions about the natural world and our place in it. But when it comes to matters of faith and science, many people mistakenly believe that the Catholic Church has a contentious relationship with the sciences, which could not be further from the truth! As I mentioned in an earlier chapter, according to a survey conducted by St. Mary Press and the Center for Applied Research in the Apostolate titled *Going, Going, Gone: The Dynamics of Disaffiliation in Young Catholics,* the typical age for a young person to leave the Catholic faith was made around age 13 but as young as 10. Nearly two-thirds of those surveyed, or 63 percent, said that they stopped being Catholic between the ages of 10 and 17. Another 23 percent said they left the faith before age 10. Staggeringly, only 13 percent said that they were ever likely to return to the Catholic Church.

What Research Reveals

Many of the interviews revealed that many young people decided to disassociate with the Catholic faith because of their perceived understanding that Catholicism does not support a scientific worldview. As one interviewee stated in the survey: "Catholic beliefs aren't based on fact. Everything is hearsay from back before anything could be documented, so nothing can be disproved, but it certainly shouldn't be taken seriously." Another said that "religion is in complete contradiction with the rational and scientific world, and to continue to subscribe to a religion would be hypocritical."

Clearly young people are hungering for meaning and desire to understand their world, including the place of science within it. Navigating tough issues through the lens of our faith can instill in our children a greater sense of confidence about their faith, especially when it comes to issues of faith and science. So how can you as a parent have a thoughtful discussion with your child about science? Here are some guiding principles:

- **Acknowledge your child's interest in science as a positive and good thing.** Children have a natural curiosity about the world and how it works. Many parents find their children progress from being interested in dinosaurs to the solar system, rocks, gems and minerals, then deeper issues such as string theory and metaphysics. Don't be afraid of questions about science; it is healthy to have an inquisitive nature about the world. Share your child's passion for learning about how the world works and welcome their curiosity as an opportunity to bring faith into your discussions.

- **Affirm that faith and science are complementary.** Science is a way of learning about the world, and faith teaches us how to live in our world, by following Jesus. As Galileo is reputed to have said, "The Bible shows the way to go to heaven, not the way the heavens go." Talk to your children as often as you can about faith and science. Help them understand that the Catholic Church teaches that faith and science are complementary. The *Catechism* affirms their harmony, and many popes have spoken positively about science. Indeed, many of the greatest scientific contributions were advanced by Catholics, including some of the saints.

- **Speak factually about the Church's positive contribution to science.** The Catholic Church founded the first universities of the world, such as the University of Bologna in Italy, founded in 1088, and the University of Salamanca in Spain in 1134. If the Catholic Church opposed science, we would expect to find no or few Catholic scientists and no sponsorship by the Catholic Church of scientific studies or institutions, right? And yet our Catholic tradition is replete with them! The Catholic Church has founded and funded scientific studies since the beginning of the university and college system. Few Catholics understand the positive contributions established by the Catholic Church to fund scientific advancements. For example, the Pontifical Academy of the Sciences is a scientific academy of the Vatican established in 1936 by Pope Pius XI to provide advice about matters of science to the Catholic Church. Academy members are among the most distinguished and accomplished scientists in the world, and it is open to those of all faiths and no faith.

- **Introduce your children in elementary and middle school to the great Catholic scientists.** Research indicates that young people are making up their minds about science and faith much earlier than the high school years. Elementary school is a particularly good time to introduce young Catholics to the rich patrimony of Catholic learning in science. Historically, Catholics are among the most important scientists of all time: Augustinian priest Gregor Mendel is considered the founder of modern genetics, and Georges Lemaître, priest and physicist, was the originator of the big bang theory. Other Catholic contributors to the sciences include Roger Bacon, William of Ockham, Leonardo da Vinci, Galileo, Louis Pasteur, Pierre Teilhard de Chardin, and Mary Celine Fasenmeyer. Do some research and share their stories in your family. Find out how their scientific discoveries were influenced by their faith.

With these principles in mind, let's turn our attention to some questions in the area of science.

Did the creation events in the Bible actually take place?
—Colby, age 9

Children are insightful and curious. As they move from thinking concretely to being able to think more abstractly, their quest for truth takes interesting turns. As parents, we often shield them from the truth until they are ready for more complex ideas. As they grow up, concepts that they thought were true (such as the Easter Bunny, the Tooth Fairy, Santa Claus) are no longer. This naturally leads them to question whether God is in the same category as other entities they cannot see. When children ask about the veracity of Bible stories, they want to know if the Bible can be trusted.

The reality is that we believe as a church that the events that took place in the Bible were real and true. But the Catholic Church objects to using the book of Genesis as a scientific text and rejects what is called fundamentalism, or a literal viewpoint on creation in the Bible. It is important to note that the creation stories in Genesis use what is called "figurative" language, instead of solely literal language, to reveal truths about God and humanity. These metaphoric stories in Genesis—such as the creation of the world in six days—express basic truths about the human condition but should not be taken literally. The *Catechism of the Catholic Church* affirms that "the account of the fall in Genesis 3 uses figurative language, but affirms a primeval event, a deed that took place at the beginning of the history of man" (*CCC* #390).

Did everyone descend from Adam and Eve?

—Nate, age 11

The question of whether the entire human race descended from two people is difficult to answer, especially because science is also evolving in its understanding of this question and the Church continues to study this issue carefully. At the heart of this question is the understanding of polygenism and monogenism. Polygenism explores whether humans descended from a pool of early human couples or from one couple as outlined in the Bible. On this, the Church has not taken a definitive stance, and Catholics are not obligated to believe that Adam and Eve were the first people as a literal historical fact. What we are called to believe are instead the truths at the heart of this story: God played an ultimate role in creation and in the creation of the human being and God created us for relationship with him.

Does the Catholic Church believe in evolution?

—Milo, age 13

We believe that God created all that is in existence and that all life develops and evolves in accordance with God's plan. Scientific theories of evolution that do not contradict Catholic teaching are to be embraced provided they allow for the spiritual dimension of creation and the human person. This is what is known as *theistic evolution*, which is also known as *evolutionary creation*. As early as 1950, Pope Pius XII indicated that biological evolution is compatible with Christian faith as outlined in the papal encyclical (or document) called *Humani generis*. All Catholic schools teach the subject of evolution.

How old is the Earth?
—*Juno, age 6*

Christina, a single mom of four children, answered this question like this: "The Earth is old but not as old as God. Scientists all the time are trying to figure out how old the Earth is exactly but only God knows."

This answer is a good one for little children. For older children, you may need to go into more detail. Scientists estimate that the Earth is somewhere around 4.54 billion years old, with the universe being around 13.8 billion years old. Some Christians espouse creationism, which is a belief that the world is only approximately 6,000 years old—this would be the approximate age of the Earth if we took creation stories and other stories in the Old Testament in a literal way. As Catholics, we emphasize that our faith and reason work together and so there is no conflict with scientific views evolving to pinpoint the beginning of the universe.

Do Catholics believe in the big bang theory?
—*Rosalita, age 12*

The big bang theory is the most widely held theory of the beginning and the evolution of the universe. It is the idea that the universe emerged as just a single point from a state of extremely high temperature, pressure, and density (the big bang) that occurred over 13 billion years ago. From this single point, the universe stretched to grow larger and continues to stretch. This theory was proposed by a Catholic priest, Georges Lemaître, in 1927. Pope Pius XII and subsequent popes verified that the big bang theory does not contradict our Catholic faith. As science learns more about the universe, we may one day see creation as a process more complex than and even quite different from the big bang. Catholics are free to keep learning as scientists learn.

Parent to Parent

Question: If my kids become interested in science, how can I teach them that faith and science go together?

—Tommy and Grace, parents of two

Answer: "Why, why, why, how, how, how, what, what, what"—I feel like our kids were constant sponges when learning about faith! Dave is a physicist, and I teach chemistry at the local high school, so science is a part of the fabric of our home life. Our kids were exposed to science at a young age because there were always documentaries on the television. Our family loves *Nova*, and we always have a stack of science books around. My best advice for parents would be to avoid "either-or" language when talking about faith and science. Don't set up an oppositional tone or position. Both can go together. Use "and" language when discussing science. "Make connections whenever you can; that way science is seen as complementary without being in conflict with our faith. Acknowledge when there are areas of tension, too. Sometimes that tension can lead to great conversations."

—Roxanne and Dave, parents of nine

Was Galileo killed for his views on science?
—Jarod, age 15

Let's clear up one thing first. Galileo Galilei died on January 8, 1642, at age 77 from an illness. He had suffered from heart palpitations and a fever for some time. He was not tortured or executed by the Catholic Church.

Why did the Church condemn Galileo?
—Barry, age 14

Galileo's life and legacy have been recast in the popular imagination as a hero who stood up to the antiscientific Catholic Church. The truth, however, as it usually is, is far more nuanced. At the time, the Catholic Church actively supported and funded scientific discoveries and hosted regular discussions on the subject. Galileo's teaching on heliocentrism (that Earth moves around the sun), which Copernicus championed, was not actually the core of the dispute with the Catholic Church, for even in 1611 a team of Jesuit astronomers had verified Galileo's claims. It is a complex issue, but it seems that Galileo got into hot water not for his scientific claims but for his theological claims, which threw the question of creation by God into dispute. Galileo was accused of heresy by the Inquisition and forced to stand trial in 1633. He was found guilty. He was then sentenced to a lifetime of house arrest and his book *Dialogue*, which contained his findings, was banned. However, in 1992, at the Pontifical Academy of Sciences, St. Pope John Paul II formally declared that Galileo was right and that the Inquisition, while acting in good faith, was in error.

Can you be a Catholic and believe in aliens?

—*Fatima, age 12*

The Catholic Church holds no official teaching on extraterrestrial life or what are often referred to as aliens. But speculation among theologians has been fertile ground for much discussion for years. The Jesuit brother Guy Consolmagno is head of the Vatican Observatory and is sometimes called "the pope's astronomer." In an interview in the May 2012 issue of *US Catholic*, Consolmagno indicated that the Catholic tradition has no issue with the idea of intelligent life on other planets. He states: "I think we recognize that if they're from Alpha Centauri or from the next galaxy over, they're still God's creation. It's all God's creation! If we ever find intelligent life, we'll have an interesting dialogue about the nature of the incarnation." So, you certainly can be a Catholic and believe in aliens!

What does the Church think about genetic engineering?
—Katerina, age 16

The subject of genetic engineering is complex and multifaceted. In 2020 the new *Directory for Catechesis* was released, and it addresses a whole host of issues, such as genetic engineering and bioethics. In its sections 373–378 it outlines four fundamental elements to be considered with respect to bioethical issues. It says: "God is the initial and ultimate reference of life, from its conception to natural death; the person is always unity of spirit and body; science is at the service of the person; life must be accepted in any condition, because it is redeemed by the paschal mystery of Jesus Christ." On the subject of genetic engineering, the *Directory* states that genetic engineering can be a good therapeutic intervention as long as it is consistent with God's plan for the human person.

Why is the Church against euthanasia and assisted suicide?
—Madlyn, age 17

We all have endured some kind of suffering. Whether it is the anguish of infertility, the almost unbearable loss of a spouse or a child, the humiliation of being fired from a job we love, or the ongoing struggle of a health situation, suffering seems to come in all shapes and sizes. It is part of who we are as people.

Many times, it's easier to suffer ourselves rather than watch a loved one suffer. We want to take the pain away and yet we cannot. In such circumstances it can seem more merciful to hasten death since it seems kinder, and the person is "put out of pain." But the pain is not ours to bear or ours to take away. We cannot deliberately end the life of another. Only God is the creator of life.

It's important to get our definitions straight. *Euthanasia* is the deliberate ending of the life of a person who is suffering with an incurable and painful disease or who is in an irreversible coma. *Assisted suicide* is when someone else helps a patient to die; *physician-assisted suicide* (PAS) is suicide that is assisted by a physician or other health-care provider. The Catholic Church takes a clear and firm stance against euthanasia or any type of assisted suicide, stating that "whatever its motives and means, direct euthanasia consists in putting an end to the lives of handicapped, sick, or dying persons. It is morally unacceptable" (*CCC* #2277). The Church affirms the dignity of each person, and in the same way the Church opposes capital punishment, it views ending a life prematurely as deeply wrong. It is important to note that the Church does allow and encourage palliative care that addresses pain and alleviates suffering.

This is a deeply contentious issue and is facing significant legal debate and challenges all across the world. As you engage this subject with your child, talk about the entire issue, including cases where government authority has overridden the wishes of, for example, a person in a coma or the wishes of family and parents with regard to their own children.

What about keeping someone alive for a long time that is in a coma?
—Shanique, age 13

Again, the Catholic Church sees science and medical care as necessary and important. When it comes to keeping the human person alive, the Church believes that all measures ought to be considered in the light of how they support the life of the person.

There are two kinds of care that need to be explained in a situation like this: ordinary and extraordinary. Ordinary means of care involve basic elements of human survival and comfort that all people have a right to. Ordinary care includes food, water, bathing, human contact, and other basic items that do not cause the person an undue burden and help a person to survive. Extraordinary care involves medical interventions that are more invasive, provide minimal benefit to the patient, and are expensive or very burdensome. For example, a cancer patient may not want to go through an expensive and exhausting procedure that will provide a few extra months of life; instead, they choose to let nature take its course, and this is morally acceptable. In the case of the person who is in a coma, ordinary means of care should be provided, and to take someone away to hasten or speed up their death is considered wrong.

When a friend of mine lost both of her parents in a relatively short period of time, she implored me: "Set up a system now to provide for your children in case something happens. Nobody should be in the midst of the grieving process while trying to do all this legal work—it's absolutely exhausting." This is good advice. We can make it clear to our loved ones how we want to be cared for in the case of a coma or an illness that makes it impossible for us to communicate. Such things as living wills and power of attorney can be immensely helpful. Clarifying now what we can helps family members honor and care for each other.

There is a narrative in our world that faith is irrational and irrelevant in the face of increasing scientific progress. But excessive belief in the power of scientific knowledge and methods is known as scientism. Scientism has become rampant in recent years, and those who try to raise critical issues with respect to technology and science are often labeled "out of touch." Yet we must remember that science is a tool and, when wielded in accord with God's plan for humanity, is a good thing. But science as a discipline is not morally neutral and can be used for good or bad. For example, it was scientific advancements that led to the development of nuclear technology, which contributed to the proliferation of cheap, abundant power that benefits millions of people. Unfortunately, nuclear technology also has been wielded in war, contaminated the environment, and led to a devastating loss of plant, animal, and human life when nuclear facilities have malfunctioned. As Catholics we can applaud scientific progress and maintain a deep faith consistent with God's plan for our world while being concerned when there are ethical and moral considerations that are being overlooked.

Let's now move our conversation from the world of science and outer space back to Earth. The next appendix explores how to live our faith through the lens of what is called the liturgical year.

Take It Home

Key Takeaways

- Faith and science are complementary.
- Elementary school is a particularly good time to introduce young Catholics to conversations about faith and science.
- Historically, many Catholics who were important scientists, some at the forefront of their areas of study.
- God created all that is in existence, and all life develops and evolves in accordance with God's plan.
- Catholics can embrace scientific theories of evolution provided that they allow for the spiritual dimension of creation and the human person.
- The Catholic Church has no official teaching on extraterrestrial life or aliens.
- The Church encourages compassionate palliative care that alleviates suffering but does not support euthanasia, which is the deliberate taking of the life of another who is suffering.

Reflect and Journal

Using the chart below as a springboard, list some topics of natural curiosity that your children have. The ideas are not exhaustive, so please feel free to add your own. Make a note of any ways that you can connect this interest to the Catholic faith. Perhaps it is through the life of a saint, a visit to a museum of science, or a particular story or video.

Area of Interest	Connection with Our Catholic Faith
Dinosaurs	
Solar system, planets and galaxies	
Biology	
UFOs and extraterrestrials	
Satellite and rocket technology	
Geology, minerals, natural specimens	
Human and animal biology	
Artificial intelligence	

Practice: Explore!

Consider visiting a science museum with the express purpose of opening a dialogue in your family about faith and science.

Many schools have a science fair. Use this opportunity to talk about your child's project in the light of their faith.

Pray: With the Scientists

Pray as a family with some quotes from scientists.

Guglielmo Marconi (1874–1937) was the inventor of wireless telegraphy and the radio, and he won the Nobel Prize in 1909. He stated: "I declare it proudly: I am a believer. I believe in the power of prayer, and I believe not only as a Catholic, but also as a scientist."

Thomas A. Edison (1847–1931) is one of the most famous American scientists. He is reputed to have held over 1,200 patents in many different areas, including science, engineering, and physics. He said: "My utmost respect and admiration to all the engineers, especially the greatest of them all: God."

Recommended Resources

For you: The Magis Center, founded by the Jesuit scholar and priest Fr. Robert Spitzer, has excellent books, videos, and other resources for parents, children, and educators about the world of faith and science. Visit www.magiscenter.com for more information.

For your children: The book *Brilliant! 25 Catholic Scientists, Mathematicians, and Supersmart People,* by David and Jaclyn Warren, introduces children to many Catholics behind some of the greatest discoveries in science and math.

Appendix 1

Celebrating Angels, Mary, and the Saints

There are all sorts of ways to live the liturgical life, to go through daily life connected with the Church and our living faith. The domestic church is critically important, and we can learn how to live our faith more fully in unity with the wider universal church. To help us do this, the church orders the calendar year in such a way that time is punctuated with a greater depth and sacredness, leading us to worship God more fully. This is known as the liturgical calendar. Living in harmony with the liturgical cycle of the year is an important part of Catholic life.

Liturgical Smells, Bells, and Seasons

Your children may not pose questions about the liturgical year; after all, days and seasons don't seem as crucial to understand as the moral and theological issues covered in previous chapters. However, the more they learn about and live the church calendar, the more grounded in the Christian faith they will become. They will understand faith life as not simply things to do or not do but also a way of moving intentionally through time and seasons. They will, with each passing year, feel more familiar with the rhythms and traditions. Faith itself will feel more and more natural, hopeful, and joyful.

So a little theology on the liturgical year since it does not synchronize with the calendar year. Just as the seasons change, there is a beautiful rhythm to the liturgical year of the Church. This helps us understand how life transitions and the rituals of the Church prepare us to receive Jesus in every season. Time itself has long been marked in the West by Jesus' life, death, and resurrection. "BC" stands for the English phrase "before Christ," and "AD" stands for the Latin phrase *anno domini*, which means "in the year of the Lord"—which marks time since the year Jesus was born. The word *liturgy* comes from the Greek word *leitourgia*, which refers to a form of public worship or ritual. The liturgical year consists of a seasonal cycle and a sanctoral cycle—these are called the Proper of Time and the Proper of Saints—in which we celebrate certain feast days. The liturgical year does not correspond to our regular calendar but instead begins with the season of Advent and consists of six seasons as follows:

Advent is a time of waiting and joyful preparation for the birth of Jesus at Christmas. Advent begins four Sundays before Christmas and is usually between three and four weeks long.

Christmas is not just one day (December 25) but several weeks of celebrating the incarnation and the birth of Jesus. Christmas begins with the birth of Jesus (the Nativity) and includes the celebration of the Epiphany and concludes with the baptism of the Lord. The exact length of the Christmas season varies from year to year.

Lent is a season of preparation for Easter. Lent begins on Ash Wednesday and ends on Holy Thursday afternoon. If Sundays are excluded from the count, Lent lasts for forty days.

The Sacred Paschal Triduum is considered the three holiest days of the Church's year, during which the suffering, death, and resurrection of Jesus are recalled. The word *Triduum* comes from a Latin root meaning "three days." The Triduum is celebrated from Holy Thursday evening to Easter Sunday evening as follows:

- Holy Thursday we remember the Last Supper of Jesus with the disciples. The liturgy includes "the washing of the feet" and time for adoration of the Blessed Sacrament.
- Good Friday commemorates the crucifixion death (sometimes called the Passion) and burial of Jesus. The word passion comes from the Latin word *passionem*, meaning "suffering" or "enduring."
- Holy Saturday commemorates Jesus' time in the tomb when a great silence came upon the earth.
- Easter Vigil is celebrated Saturday after sunset or Sunday before dawn. This liturgy begins the celebration of the Resurrection. It includes the lighting of the Easter fire and the Easter candle. Easter Sunday commemorates the day of Jesus' resurrection, and the liturgy includes a sprinkling rite and the renewal of our baptismal promises.

Easter includes fifty days of celebration of the resurrection of Jesus and the sending forth of the Holy Spirit at Pentecost.

Ordinary Time is divided into two sections—a period of four to eight weeks after Christmastime and another period lasting about six months after the season of Easter until the Solemnity of Christ the King.

Together these seasons provide a rhythm for understanding God, grounding us in God's plan for our lives, and moving us more deeply into the mystery of his love. Living liturgically does not have to be an arduous task but can be a series of small steps that move us more gradually into the liturgical seasons. One of the easiest ways you can live in accordance with the Church's liturgical season is to incorporate the colors and meanings of the liturgical seasons into your home.

A Guide to the Liturgical Seasons, Colors, and Their Meanings

Liturgical Season	Typical Time of Year	Color	Meaning of Color
Advent	December	Blue and purple. On the fourth Sunday of Advent, the color rose is worn.	Preparation, waiting, sacrifice
Christmas	December–January	White and gold	Glory, birth, joy
The Sacred Paschal Triduum	March or April	Red and purple	Penance, preparation, sacrifice
Easter	March or April	White and gold	Glory, joy, light, rebirth
Ordinary Time	4–8 weeks after Christmas and 6 months after Easter season until the Solemnity of Christ the King	Green	Life, hope, anticipation, growth

The primary colors in the liturgical calendar are red, white, gold, violet, green, and black. The liturgical calendar is punctuated by other colors at certain times of the year such as on Gaudete Sunday and Laetare Sunday, when the color rose (not pink!) is worn. If you struggle to understand the difference between rose and pink, just remember that Jesus rose from the dead, he didn't "pink" from it as one of my priest friends reminds his parishioners! Gaudete Sunday takes place on the Third Sunday of Advent, and Laetare Sunday takes place on the fourth Sunday of Lent. The words *Gaudete* and *Laetare* mean "rejoice," as both days' themes come from the entrance antiphon that is a part of the Introductory Rite at Mass, "Rejoice, Jerusalem, and all who love her. Be joyful, all who were in mourning; exalt and be satisfied at her consoling breast" (Isa. 66:10–11).

Now that we have covered the main points of the liturgical year, let's move to some ways that you can live in harmony with the Church's liturgical feast days and celebrations. In this next section, I share some ideas from families throughout the world that can inspire you to live more fully *la vida litúrgica*, beginning with cultivating a home altar or prayer space.

A Family Prayer Space or Home Altar

It is important to have a space for prayer in your home. It doesn't have to be a whole room or something formal and grand and can be a simple yet meaningful space for you to gather alone or with your family.

Where: While prayer can take place in any room in your home (and it should!), consider setting aside a special nook or a dedicated space that feels a bit more sacred.

What: You might choose the top of a shelf, a mantel, a desk, or a section on the top of your buffet or cabinet. Group together special items that are sacred and meaningful to you. You can set out some battery-operated candles, the Bible, a crucifix, or specific images or pictures that you want your family to focus on. You could include a piece of framed Scripture or your family picture. You can place images of family, friends, and pets who have passed away and remember the day of their passing each year. Consider placing baptism certificates or baptism candles in this space. Or group together your family rosary beads. You are limited only by your imagination!

How: Make a point of gathering for regular prayer in this space. It could be in the morning for a few moments or after your dinner or every night before people go to bed. You can change out the space for the different liturgical seasons to help your family move with the Church through the liturgical year. During Ordinary Time, you can have a simple green cloth on your prayer table; during Lent, a purple cloth. This way, the domestic Church and the universal Church are connected. You can pray *lectio divina* on the upcoming Gospel reading a few days before Mass. You can also pray *lectio divina* with your children during anxious times, such as when they will take a test or have surgery coming up. *Lectio divina* is an ancient way of reading the Scriptures, as we discussed previously. The "Take It Home" section for this chapter includes a simple *lectio divina* that you can pray alone or with your family.

Regardless of what you put in your prayer space or how you use it, make sure that you and your family visit it often. That way it doesn't become outdated but rather incorporated into the rhythm of your family life. Speaking of the rhythm of family life, let's now turn our attention to the larger family of saints into which we are all baptized in Christ: the saints and their feast days.

Feast Days Associated with the Virgin Mary

Many images of Mary depict her holding the infant Jesus in her arms with Jesus facing toward us. She holds up her son so that we can see him clearly. This is a central truth of Mary's life: she always points not to herself but to her Son, the one who died for each of us and seeks to bring all people to his Father. This is also our mission: not to point to ourselves but to Jesus, who presents himself to each of us and invites us into relationship with him. In our families, we try to hold up Jesus for one another, and Mary can be a powerful guide for us. There are many ways to celebrate Mary's life as there are a multitude of Marian feast days celebrated throughout the year. The principal feasts are as follows:

- The Solemnity of Mary, celebrated January 1—a holy day of obligation
- The Presentation of Our Lord in the Temple, February 2
- The Annunciation, March 25
- The Assumption, August 15—a holy day of obligation
- The Immaculate Conception, December 8—a holy day of obligation

Depending on your culture and family heritage, there are other important feast days, such as Our Lady of Guadalupe (December 12), Our Lady of Lourdes (February 11), and Our Lady of Fatima (May 13). You may choose to celebrate a few feast days or incorporate all of them into your family routine. It is important that you prepare your family for the upcoming feast day by talking about what the feast day is about. For example, as we discussed earlier, the Feast of the Immaculate Conception does not refer to the conception of Jesus in the womb, as many believe, but about the immaculate conception of Mary herself in the womb of her mother, Anne. The immaculate conception does not mean a virgin birth for Mary; she was conceived by Joachim and Anne in the natural way. But Mary herself did not inherit sin, nor did she sin throughout her whole life. That's what this special feast day is all about. Have a conversation about the heart of the feast day and how we can live out what the feast day means.

In addition to preparing for the feast day, here are a few other simple ways to celebrate Mary:

- Blue is the color traditionally associated with Mary. Consider displaying on your home altar a statue of Mary on a simple blue background or scarf.
- During the month of May, you could have your own "May crowning" and place a crown of flowers on Mary's head.
- October is the month dedicated to the Rosary, so consider making a special effort to pray the rosary during this time.
- Celebrate with food! Some families incorporate treats into their family celebrations. Preston and Eliza, parents of eight, said: "On the major feast days of Mary, our family goes to Mass and then we gather to eat blue cupcakes to celebrate the day. We make them the evening before, and this simple tradition has become a favorite of our family."

- On the feast of Our Lady of Guadalupe, display roses on your home altar, learn about St. Juan Diego, and eat some of the traditional Mexican foods associated with this feast day.
- Play Marian hymns throughout the year but especially on special days.
- Plant a small Marian garden. There are many plants associated with Mary, such as roses and lilies. Other flowers include marigold, which means "Mary's gold"; lavender, which is known as "Mary's drying plant"; and daisies, which have an alternative name of "Mary's star."

Family life can feel overwhelming at the best of times without adding other things to the mix, so in keeping with the simplicity of Mary's life and her deep devotion to God, keep it simple when you find ways to honor her! Now that we have covered some aspects of feast days associated with the Blessed Mother, let's move on to discussing other feast days.

Celebrating Other Feast Days

Many opportunities for us to live as Catholics are already ingrained in the fabric of society, although we need to be conscious of celebrating the seasons in a way that honors God and not just give in to the consumerism that sometimes undergirds these special celebrations. For example, Valentine's Day is widely celebrated throughout the world with candy and flowers as the holiday of romance, but at its root it is about remembering the life of St. Valentine, who died as a martyr for his Catholic faith. The same is true of Easter: it has become synonymous with spring flowers, bunnies, and pastel colors, and while we can bring some of the more worldly elements into our homes, we need to keep the focus on our faith and the saints at the heart of the celebration. Here's a roundup of a few ways to celebrate some of the more popular saints.

St. Valentine's Day, February 14

The saint we celebrate on February 14 is known officially by the church as St. Valentine of Rome, to differentiate him from other saints who were also called St. Valentine. You might choose to celebrate St. Valentine of Viterbo on November 3 or St. Valentine of Raetia on January 7. Or how about honoring the only female St. Valentine (Valentina), a virgin martyred in Palestine on July 25, in the year 308? Pick one and strive to get to know that saint.

Send a card or flowers or chocolate if you want to. But do so as an expression of faith.

St. Valentine is the patron of lovers and marriages but also beekeepers, those suffering from epilepsy, from the plague, those who faint, and those who travel frequently. How about remembering all those who suffer from epilepsy and offering up a prayer for their healing? Or for those who have been disappointed in love? You could decorate with some hearts but also bees as well.

St. Patrick's Day, March 17

This is a day to honor Ireland's most famous saint, who devoted himself tirelessly to prayer, fasting, and walking in faith with the Irish people. There are ways to bring this day alive for children that involve creativity and fun, but we should not forget that this is a day to celebrate our Catholic identity. I spent twenty-three years of my life growing up in Ireland before I moved to the United States, and some of the traditions I see today associated with St. Patrick's Day are so devoid of the real meaning of St. Patrick's Day as to be almost comical. This includes leaving out leprechaun traps and gold coins to catch leprechauns, which have nothing to do with St. Patrick. People in Ireland who celebrate St. Patrick's Day are more likely to serve a meal that includes cabbage, cauliflower, and carrots (colors of Ireland's flag), wear buttons with emblems of a harp or shamrock, or pin real shamrocks to clothing on that day. They might sing (in Irish) Patrick's famous "Breastplate Prayer."

There are two primary sources of the life and public ministry of St. Patrick written by his own hand: his *Confessions* and *The Letter to King Coroticus*. To make this day more meaningful, read a paragraph or line from his *Confessions* and meditate upon the words and prayers he wrote, especially around St. Patrick's Day. There are other rich and varied ways that you can celebrate the life of St. Patrick: by renewing your baptismal promises, by praying St. Patrick's prayers, by enjoying a special meal together as a family, and by "unceasingly" giving thanks to God, who often pardons our "folly and carelessness," according to St. Patrick.

St. Nicholas, December 6

When German, Polish, Belgian, and Dutch immigrants came to the United States, they brought with them their faith and the tradition of St. Nicholas, whose feast day is December 6. Here's how Pawel and Ewa, who are originally from Poland, celebrate St. Nick: "On the eve of St. Nicholas's Day, everyone in our family leaves shoes down by the fireplace. We used to leave shoes outside our bedroom doors, but we have light sleepers and so the fireplace works better for us. We fill the shoes with an orange, some chocolate coins, and a small toy or pack of collectible cards. Nothing extravagant. We all participate, everyone gets something from St. Nicholas, and on his feast day we read a story about his life while enjoying our gifts."

While today St. Nicholas is often depicted with reindeer, in traditional legends he was known to ride a donkey. Some families leave a carrot or a piece of hay in the shoes for the donkey.

Celebrating Guardian Angels and the Saints

Archangels, September 29

There are three archangels celebrated by the Catholic Church: St. Gabriel, St. Michael, and St. Raphael.

St. Gabriel is the patron saint of telecommunication workers, radio broadcasters, postal workers, and messengers. He is particularly associated with the Annunciation because he appeared to Mary and also to Zechariah, both visits to announce a birth. The name *Gabriel* means "power of God."

St. Michael is the patron of the church and of grocers, soldiers, doctors, mariners, first responders, and police. The St. Michael the Archangel prayer has increasingly become popular in recent years. He is particularly invoked to protect us against evil.

St. Raphael is the patron saint of travelers, blind people, nurses, pharmacists, physicians, and those who are ill. The name *Raphael* means "God heals" and so he is particularly associated with healing.

Guardian Angels, October 2

This day honors the guardian angels who are assigned to enlighten, strengthen, and guide each of us. We often invoke their protection physically, but their main job is to guard us against any kind of spiritual harm. You can celebrate the feast days associated with the archangels and the angels in a whole host of ways. If you have not recited the Angel of God prayer, this feast day is a good day to refamiliarize yourself with that classic prayer. Angel and Joey, who are parents of four children, love to celebrate the angels. Angel indicates that they celebrate the feast days of the angels with food such as angel hair pasta and angel food cake.

Patron Saints

If your child is named after a patron saint, celebrating the life of the saint on their feast day is an easy place to start living more liturgically. Even if your child or children were named for family members, this can be a wonderful way to explore the Catholic faith by finding out about all the saints who also bore that name. For example, if you have a son named Joseph who was named after his grandfather, you could have a special celebration on the feast of St. Joseph (March 19) or the feast of St. Joseph the Worker (May 1).

If your child has a name that does not correlate with the name of a saint, you and your family could spend time picking a patron saint by focusing on what the saint is a patron of and finding correlations with the personality of your children. Xavier did this with his family: "My daughter Clarita was not named for a saint but instead for my mother. While we did explore the life of St. Clare of Assisi, as the name *Clarita* is closely related to *Clare*, ultimately Clarita was not drawn to her life. But Clarita is a very musical child and plays three different instruments. We were led to St. Cecilia, who is the patron saint of music. Clarita was very drawn to her as a saint, and we now celebrate St. Cecilia's feast day with lots of music in our house and a special cake."

Other ways to include patron saints in your family include researching what saints are associated with the day of your birth or a meaningful date in your family.

Family Litany of Saints: It can be a wonderful project to compile all the saints associated with your family and pray them together as a litany in the following format:

> St. Joseph, pray for us.
> St. Cecilia, pray for us.
> St. Francis Xavier, pray for us . . .

Take It Home

Key Takeaways

- The liturgical year is how the church orders the calendar year, leading us to worship God more fully.
- The liturgical year begins with the season of Advent and consists of six seasons: Advent, Christmas, Lent, the Sacred Paschal Triduum, Easter, and Ordinary Time.
- The primary colors in the liturgical calendar are red, white, gold, violet, green, and black. Additional colors such as rose are added on feast days.
- Having a dedicated space in the home where the family can gather for prayer is important in helping children understand the liturgical year.
- *Lectio divina* is an ancient method of praying the Scriptures.
- Mary's mission is also our mission: not to point to ourselves but to point our entire lives to Jesus.

Reflect and Journal

Do you and your family live in attunement with the liturgical seasons? What seasons are celebrated well in your family? What could use a little work?

Does your family have a devotion to the Blessed Mother? How is she a part of your life? The spiritual life of your family? How can the life of the Blessed Mother inspire greater reverence in your family?

What the Liturgical Calendar Means to Our Family

Season	Reflect
Advent	
Christmas	
Ordinary Time after the Epiphany	
Lent	
Easter	
Ordinary Time after Pentecost	

Practice: Living with the Saints

Follow the saints, because those who follow them
will become saints.
—Pope St. Clement I

Staying close to the lives of the saints can help us grow in holiness. There are various excellent websites devoted to learning more about the saints and their lives. One way to deepen your appreciation of the saints is to try one of the many "patron saints generator" websites. There are many to choose from if you search online. With just a few clicks, you will be assigned a particular saint and given background information, prayers, and other resources. Generating a patron saint for each of your children would be an excellent way of encouraging frequent reading and reflection on the lives of the saints.

You could have a family patron saint, in addition to each child focusing on a particular saint. This could be the saint after whom they were named, the saint they picked at their confirmation, or a saint they simply relate to the most.

Consider family names. Are there recurring names in your family that reference a particular saint?

What confirmation name did you choose? Why did you choose that name?

Would you choose the same confirmation name today? Why or why not?

Who are your favorite saints? Why?

What are some ways you can deepen your love for the saints?

Is there someone in your life whom you would describe as a "living saint"? For what reasons?

Pray: *Lectio Divina*

The ancient practice of *lectio divina* arose out of the monastic tradition of praying with the Scriptures, not as texts to be studied but as the living word of God that leads us to deeper communion with God and one another. There are five steps in *lectio divina*:

1. Reading, or *lectio*, of the text. What does the text reveal about God? In this stage we are seeking to understand God's meaning in the Scriptures.

2. Meditation, or *meditatio*, on the text. What does the text reveal to us? This stage situates us in the text as if we were participating or represented in the particular passage.

3. Prayer, or *oratio*. What is our prayer or response to the Lord? In this step we are drawing closely to the Lord and speak to him in our own words as we have been moved by the encounter with his word.

4. Contemplation, or *contemplatio*. What conversion is the Lord asking of us? An encounter with God in his word leads us to a transformation whereby we strive to conform our will to his.

5. Response, or the *actio*, which completes our prayerful reading of the text. In this step we consider what God asks of us in response to his word.

In *Evangelii gaudium*, a document written by Pope Francis, he urges us to pray with Scripture by asking the following questions:

- What "jumped" out at me?
- What touched my heart the most?
- What areas do I need to seek further understanding on?
- What should I pray about next?

Recommended Resources

For you: Voices of the Saints: A 365-Day Journey with Our Spiritual Companions, by Bert Ghezzi, introduces readers to 365 holy men and women, from the best known to some of the most obscure. This engaging book includes biographical profiles, quotations from the saints, meditations, and prayers.

For your children: Introducing your children to the Bible can be pretty simple with Amy Welborn's *Book of Bible Stories: 60 Scripture Stories Every Catholic Child Should Know.* This beautiful collection of warm and engaging stories for families is arranged in a uniquely Catholic way, based on the liturgical year and the order in which they are proclaimed during the Mass.

Appendix 2

Celebrating Advent, Lent, and Easter

As parents, we want to do the best that we can for our children, and we often feel guilty that we're not good enough or must do extraordinary things to keep faith at the heart of the family home. Not so. In this appendix I'm going to continue sharing with you many simple ideas to live liturgically. Again, these ideas have been suggested by parents throughout the country and can be integrated into your family with little to no fuss or stress. Mary and Nick remind us that simplicity can be embraced, and she shares how she approaches life in a blended family with three children.

> I have found that instilling faith in children is much less formal than I expected. Before having children, I believed rigorous catechesis and learning Latin would inspire lasting faith. Turns out, it happens in the most mundane moments: blessings at school drop-offs, praying for friends and family in need, sharing the meaning behind my favorite scriptures and hymns at Mass. The challenge of parenting Catholic kids, in my experience, comes down to Jesus' challenge for us all: to have faith like a child. My son connects so easily to gratitude for simple pleasures, marveling at creation, trusting God and talking to him as our friend, and asking for help. Instilling faith happens at their level, on their time, and I'm continually shocked at how my child is inspired by the lessons he learns when I'm not trying at all. Everything I say and do is a lesson to my child in Christian living, and I am crushed

under the weight of that responsibility, especially coupled with my spectacular diversity in shortcomings. In my parenting, I'm really coming to appreciate the idea of the domestic church; the sacredness of family life, the first place God happens. Raising Catholic kids doesn't come with a textbook, timeline, or parent handbook (though we wish it did!), but the great news is it doesn't have to.

In this appendix we go through some of the major liturgical seasons and provide some simple ways that you can make these seasons more special, starting with Advent. This may feel like ideation overload, but, again, choose one or two simple things to do that fit with your family and incorporate them into your own traditions.

Advent

The word *Advent* is derived from the Latin word *adventus*, which means "coming." As such, Advent is not just a prelude or warmup for Christmas. Instead, at a time when the world wants us to hurry, to shop, and to busy ourselves with preparations for Christmas, Advent invites us to pause, to wonder, to savor. The Scriptures invite us to greater attentiveness and awareness of how God is moving in our midst.

Growing up in Ireland, I remember how common it was to see a single candle placed in the windows of homes throughout the Christmas season. This tradition has spread across the world, and yet many people have forgotten the rich meaning and symbolism behind it. Where does it come from and what does it mean?

In Ireland, the single lit candle in the window symbolized a time when the Irish were heavily persecuted and oppressed for their faith. During the era of what was known as the Penal Laws, it was forbidden for Catholics to gather publicly for prayer, and the public practice of Mass was outlawed. However, during this time, the Irish found ways to secretly practice their faith without drawing the negative attention of the authorities. During the time of the Penal Laws, priests moved from village to village under the cover of darkness to avoid being arrested, and "safe houses" were designated as places where priests could rest and offer Mass before moving on again.

On Christmas Eve, a single lit candle was placed in the window of a home that was easily visible to wandering priests. At its heart, the candle was a beacon of hope and hospitality, indicating a home that was welcoming of all strangers but particularly priests who wandered the highways and byways of Ireland.

Any family who wished to welcome a priest safely into their home and avail of the sacraments would place a single lit candle in the window and leave the door unlatched. If the family was questioned about the practice by the English authorities, they would explain that the candle was a symbol of their welcome to Joseph and Mary as they wandered on Christmas Eve looking for a place to rest and give birth to the baby Jesus. The candle in the window became synonymous with providing a safe place for travelers and those without a home.

José and Antonia, parents of two who immigrated to the United States, incorporated this simple practice into their Advent tradition to remember all those who wander like the Holy Family.

> Our family came to the United States seeking asylum during Advent. Our passage was complicated and stressful, and our family was assisted by a nun from Ireland. At the center where we were housed, she had put a candle in her window. We asked her why and she talked to us about this tradition. Once we got settled, we adopted it for our family as a light for all those who are looking for a safe place to call home.

In addition to the candle in the window, here are some other simple ways to celebrate Advent:

- **Advent wreath.** Decorate your own Advent wreath and gather each evening or every week to light a candle, read Scripture, and pray together. The lighting of the Advent wreath helps us remain faithful to the meaning and purpose of this sacred time.

- **Advent calendar.** Many children receive Advent calendars that include a small square of chocolate. You can also consider making your own calendar.

- **Jesse tree.** Create your own or buy a simple Jesse tree and learn the stories of Jesus' family. Each day focuses on a different passage from the Bible, from the book of Genesis to the birth of Jesus.

- **Music.** Some of the most beautiful hymns in the Catholic tradition are reserved for Advent. While there is nothing wrong with playing Christmas music during this time, make a special effort to listen to Advent music.

- **Decorating.** Rather than decorating for Christmas and skipping through Advent, consider decorating your house and Christmas tree in stages so that the meaning of Advent can unfold.

- **Advent angels.** Here is another simple tradition to encourage children to pray for one another. Each person in your house secretly chooses the name of someone within the family (or outside the family) to pray for. You can also incorporate random acts of kindness into this activity. Family members reveal their identity to each other only on Christmas morning. Some families incorporate a guessing game in which family members are given clues and they try to guess which person is their Advent angel. If you have small children in your family, consider purchasing or making a small doll (an Advent angel) for your children. This would be a wonderful small gift from the parish to families in religious education or those children in Catholic schools. It is the job of the Advent angel to guide the child toward Christmas. Each night a Scripture passage is read, and the family gathers to talk about what their Advent angel has shown them that day about Christ.

- While it is tempting to skip right to Christmas, staying true to our Catholic faith means also being true to the marking of sacred time. Explaining the meaning and purpose of Advent helps us wait and prepare for the birth of Jesus Christ. Our prayer helps us to do that during Advent. So does our music. During the season of Advent, we watch, we wait, and we prepare. And when Christmas comes, as it always does, it is so much sweeter and more meaningful for our waiting.

Christmas

As the seasons change, so does the rhythm of the Church's year. This helps us all to appreciate the beauty of time and God's presence in our lives. However, keeping pace with sacred time is becoming much more difficult these days. It can seem that this time of year is one enormous Halloween-Thanksgiving-Christmas extravaganza. Keeping Christ not just in Christmas but at the center of our lives can be an uphill battle, but it is worth it. Many families have very specific traditions with respect to their culture and heritage when celebrating Christmas that involve food, music, art, and prayer.

Here are a couple of other simple ways to keep Christ at the center of Christmas. None of these involves any money, but all will add quality to your family celebrations, and that is priceless.

Christmas Mass. Christmas Mass is a great opportunity to see people we don't always see at church. Talk about this as a family and how you can make other people feel welcome during this special time of year. If your children are at an appropriate age, consider volunteering together to open doors to the church at the Christmas Mass. When children are greeters, it can make quite an impression! Prepare yourself and your family before Christmas Mass by sharing the readings and listening for a new insight about the birth of Jesus. Following Mass, share one thing that will help you focus more deeply on the real meaning of Christmas. On Christmas Eve, pray a family blessing of the manger using one found easily online or in your own words.

Bedtime. Make bedtime during the Christmas season meaningful. For families that read stories to their children before bedtime, instead of reading books such as *How the Grinch Stole Christmas* (a great story but make room for other stories), instead read the Nativity story and other Christmas-themed stories and reflect as a family. Ask questions such as "What difference has Jesus made to my life?" or "How has Jesus' birth changed the world?" Listen attentively, especially as children share their thoughts. Close your storytelling with prayer.

The Christmas Manger. My friend Mary Beth and her husband Mike, parents of two, shared this beautiful tradition with me:

> My family has some great traditions on Christmas Eve. We unwrap the baby Jesus figure (from the nativity scene) and place him in the manger. (My mom always wraps it because Jesus is our first present and God's gift to us.) We all kneel in front of the manger and sing "O Come Let Us Adore Him." Then we all quietly offer Jesus a "Christmas gift"—maybe a small sacrifice, loving act toward someone, or resolution for the future. We also have a birthday cake for Jesus on Christmas Day and sing "Happy Birthday." Last, we have a toast for Jesus, with nonalcoholic sparkling wine for the kids.

The Christmas Letter. Consider this lovely tradition shared by Colm and Fiona, parents of three:

> A couple of years ago, I found a Christmas card that my mother wrote to me as a teenager. Her words were and remain the most beautiful gift to me, especially since she has passed

away. In her memory, I write each of my children a letter every Christmas Eve telling them what I love about them, what I notice about their personalities as they grow, and how much their father and I pray for them. I put the Christmas letters in their stockings, and we read them on Christmas evening. Afterward, I collect them all and keep them in a special binder for each child, which I add to every year. Someday, I plan to give this to them all at once as a Christmas gift.

Parent to Parent

Question: What are some simple ways to develop Christmas traditions that aren't expensive or elaborate?

—Hannah, mom of one

Answer: We read the Christmas Story together on Christmas Eve and give each kid a part to read. You could also consider doing a family blessing of the Manger and place the baby Jesus statue in the crib. Write a letter or prayers and place them by the Infant. Go to Mass as a family. With little kids, find a manger of their own that they can touch and rearrange. Have the Three Kings journey around different spots of the house and arrive to the crib by Epiphany.

—Krissy and Peter, parents of seven

Lent

From the joy of Christmas, we enter ordinary time and then into Lent. Lent is supposed to feel like the spiritual equivalent of a new year for us as Catholics but with one main difference. Instead of focusing entirely on our own needs and wants, as New Year's resolutions often do, Lent is a time to consider the needs of others in prayer, fasting, and almsgiving. There are a lot of ideas competing for our attention during Lent, such as particular challenges to declutter our homes, for example, but if you decide to do such a challenge or any other Lenten practice, here are three questions to ask before you do so:

1. Is this practice focused on God, others, or myself?
2. Does this practice help me fast from something that I truly struggle with?
3. Do I give, pray, and serve out of love or out of my own selfishness?

During Lent, we begin forty days of prayer, fasting, and almsgiving, and the somber and reverent tone prepares our hearts for Easter. This is an especially good time to talk about the spiritual and corporal works of mercy. If you are not familiar with the spiritual and corporal works of mercy, the "Take It Home" section at the end of this appendix includes a list of them you can use to familiarize yourself and your family. There are lots of ways to enter Lent as a family; the ideas below are just a starting point.

Ash Wednesday. Although not a holy day of obligation as many people think, Ash Wednesday begins our journey to Easter. Go as a family to receive ashes and reflect on what it means to be signed with ashes in this way. If you are comfortable, consider posting a picture to social media with your ashes, using the hashtag #ashtag.

Crown of Thorns Activity. This activity is similar to the Advent activity of placing straw in the manger every time someone in the family does something good during the season of Advent. It teaches children about the pain that Jesus endured for our sins and how sin wounds us, each other, and God. Every time a discipline of Lent is practiced (prayer, fasting, almsgiving) a thorn can be removed from the crown. Here's the recipe and directions to make a salt dough crown for Lent.

Method. Using your favorite recipe for salt dough (I use 2 cups of flour to 1 cup of salt along with ¾-1 cup of water), mix the dough together. You can substitute rye flour or whole wheat flour to make the crown darker and add cinnamon if you want it to smell nice. Mix the dough; if the dough is too sticky, add more flour; if too dry, add more liquid. Knead together until the dough comes together the consistency of bread. Leave for one hour to rest and harden. After an hour, divide the dough into three pieces and roll them into a thin snake shape so that they are suitable for braiding. On a foil- or parchment-lined cookie sheet, braid the three parts together so that they form a crown. Using toothpicks (for little ones you can snip the ends if they are too sharp), insert them all over the crown. Place in preheated three-hundred-and-fifty-degree oven and bake until golden brown. Time will vary depending on the thickness of the braid. Take out of oven and leave to cool. The dough will continue to harden the longer it is left out. You can paint the dough if you want with regular children's paints or leave it plain.

The Jelly Bean Jar. This is another good activity for counting time during Lent. Older children enjoy it as well because a sweet treat is promised at the end! Set aside two mason jars at the beginning of Lent. Fill one with jelly beans. Leave one empty. You can put a prayer on the jar signifying the various colors of the jelly beans such as this one widely available online:

"Red is for the blood he gave, green is for the grass he made. Yellow is for the sun so bright, orange is for the edge of night. Black is for the sins we made, white is for the grace He gave. Purple is for the hour of sorrow, pink is for a new tomorrow. A bag full of jelly beans, colorful and sweet, is a prayer, is a promise, is an Easter treat!"

When someone in the family completes an act of love or a sacrifice for another family member, they can put a jelly bean in the empty jar.

Hopefully by the time Easter comes, the whole family can share in the hard work won by sacrificing in this way and enjoy a sweet treat together. You can do this with each child or have one jar for the whole family.

Sacrifice. The themes of sacrifice and repentance are at the heart of Lent. Many families focus on giving up something such as candy, chocolate, or other food-related items during Lent. As our family lives by the beach on Lake Michigan, one of our Lenten family projects is to remove trash and garbage from the beach. We talk beforehand about removing rubbish from our lives during Lent and the opportunity to spring-clean our hearts for Easter. The children always enjoy this activity even if they are a little grossed out! Rubber gloves, lots of garbage bags, and a strong stomach are required!

Stations of the Cross. Attend a stations of the cross service at your parish. Or you can make your own. You can easily find printouts online for the stations. Have your children color them or decorate them. You can place them throughout the house or on the stairs and take turns reading the stations as a family.

Family Reconciliation. Lent is one of the traditional times for receiving the Sacrament of Reconciliation. Consider going as a family together.

Examination of Conscience. Consider incorporating an examination of conscience into your Lenten journey. A great resource is provided at the end of this appendix.

Lenten Food. We forgo meat on Fridays during Lent, so meatless Fridays are a simple way to mark the passage of time. "Fish-fry Fridays" are very common in Wisconsin, and various parishes have different kinds of offerings during Lent such as trout boils, smelt fries, and perch plates. Make a trip with your family to sample different kinds of fish and talk about Jesus and the disciples out fishing. Also bake pretzels, another Lenten practice.

Holy Week

Holy Week is one of the most sacred times of the year. It can feel like an intense week with the pace of the liturgies and all that is happening in the Scriptures, but it provides a multitude of fruitful opportunities to live the "smells and bells" of our faith. Holy Week is a feast for the senses. In interviewing families throughout the world to contribute ideas about Holy Week, the biggest principle I learned is this one: mimic the rhythm of what is happening at church in your home. So, for example, the songs that you hear in church during this week can be played at home, and the practices that happen at church can also take place at home. In addition to attending the Triduum, here's a roundup from various families of ideas to make Holy Week special for your family.

Palm Sunday. Turn your palm plants into works of art with palm crosses. There are lots of tutorials online. In many cultures around the world, Palm Sunday is often a day to remember those who have passed away. Consider visiting your local cemetery and tidying up your loved ones' graves or place flowers on the graves as a remembrance.

Spy Wednesday. Traditionally in many homes throughout the world, tidying and cleaning the home for Easter took place on Spy Wednesday. "Spy Wednesday" refers to Judas being the betrayer or spy of the disciples. As a family, tidy the house together or visit an elderly family member and offer to do some spring-cleaning or yard work for them. This is the day Judas betrayed Jesus for thirty pieces of silver. If you can, find silver-colored chocolate coins and place them around your prayer table. Talk about all the ways that we can betray and hurt each other and God. Talk about ways that we can make amends and love one another more deeply. Every time someone mentions a way that we can honor God, give them a chocolate silver coin. They can be eaten on this day or saved for Easter Sunday. Michele, who is a mother and grandmother, shared an interesting twist on dyeing eggs. "The last egg to dye is always the 'Judas' egg—dipped in all the colors to look brown or awful. We put the dyed eggs back into their egg cartons and close the lids. Like Jesus is in the tomb, door shut and stone in front. Then we wait."

Holy Thursday. Holy Thursday is replete with opportunities to connect the readings with life. Here are some simple ideas:

> *Food.* On Holy Thursday we hear the mention of various foods in the scriptures such as lamb and bread. Consider a special meal together such as gyros with pita bread.
>
> *Wash.* Take turns washing the feet of each other in your family. This is one of my (Julianne's) favorite traditions, and we do this every year. Our children really enjoy it. We arrange our kitchen chairs in a circle and have a basin of water and towels in the middle. My husband Wayne goes first and washes everyone's feet. Then I wash everyone's feet and last the children wash each other's feet. We add fragrant oils to the water such as frankincense and balsam. We dim the lights, light candles, and put on some Gregorian chant. We end the evening in silence (or as much as we can do with three little ones!).
>
> *Serve.* Holy Thursday is a great day to serve others who are less fortunate. Consider volunteering at a food pantry or soup kitchen or donating items for the local food pantry. Make a meal for a family that is struggling or send cards to those in the nursing homes.

Good Friday. Good Friday is an intense day for many Christians during Holy Week. The day is heavy and somber in tone and should be observed with simplicity and solemnity.

> *Silence.* Consider observing total silence between the hours of noon and three o'clock in the afternoon, or for the remainder of the day if you can. Forgo television or screens in your house to keep the mood somber and prayerful.
>
> *Reverence.* Reverence a crucifix in your home alone or together as a family.
>
> *Watch.* If you watch a movie, consider watching one such as *The Passion of the Christ* (not for younger children) or another Easter-themed movie.
>
> *Bake.* Bake hot cross buns together or ready the dough for Holy Saturday morning, being mindful that we are called to fast on Good Friday.

Easter Saturday. The Easter Vigil is one of the most beautiful liturgies that we celebrate. Beginning with the *lucernarium* (Liturgy of Light), all are naturally invited to a deeper sense of wonder and mystery. We begin with a church in darkness until light is passed from person to person throughout the church. The ancient Exultet is usually sung, and additional Scripture readings are proclaimed. There is usually incense, a sprinkling rite, not to mention newly received Catholics into the church. There's a lot going on! This can be a lengthy liturgy, though, stretching over two hours, so for very young children, preparation is key. Talking about the liturgy ahead of time is important and the reasons the liturgy is celebrated in this way.

Some families allow small children to attend the Easter Vigil in their pajamas, as they may fall asleep during the Mass. Other families bring along some "busy bags" and take along coloring books (Easter themed) or storybooks. However you choose to make this liturgy special for your family, try, try, try to attend if you can. Some families skip this liturgy because they are afraid that it is too long, but many parents have told me that the intricacy of the liturgy actually holds the attention of children in ways that we might not expect.

If you absolutely cannot attend the Easter Vigil, consider recreating some of the elements at home, such as having a bonfire outside, renewing your baptismal promises, and simulating the light passing from one family member to another either with battery-powered candles or real candles if your children are old enough.

Easter Sunday. At its heart the Bible is a love story, and of all the seasons that we celebrate as Catholics, it is Easter that reveals the depth of God's love for us. Within Easter the profound truth of our faith rests: Jesus Christ was crucified, died, and was buried and rose again on the third day—for each of us, out of love for us. It is a love that compels us to shout it from the rooftops just as Mary Magdalene did after Jesus appeared to her by the empty tomb. By our conviction of heart and mind, we can be a witness to the Resurrection just like Mary Magdalene, not just at Easter but every day. Here are some ways to keep your Easter joy.

> *Read.* If you are feeling tired and weary in your spiritual life or if your prayer life has become routine, try reading the Acts of the Apostles between Easter and Pentecost. Immerse yourself in the excitement of the disciples trying to become the church community that Jesus intended them to become with its difficult and messy relationships. Discuss your insights.
> *Reflect.* Spend a little bit of extra time in Adoration and prayer.
> *Invite.* Reach out and invite someone to Mass. According to Lifeway Research, 51 percent of Americans who don't go to church say a personal invitation from a friend or family member would be most effective in getting them to visit a local church. It isn't easy to come to Mass, particularly if you

have been away for some time. Invite your friend to come with you and your family. A simple way to do this is how Mary and Nick approach the invitations. "Our family always looks forward to Easter Sunday. I remember going as a child and loving the music and the sense of hope all around me. Our family would love for you to come with us. We are going to the ten-thirty Mass at St. John Parish on Easter Sunday; you are welcome to come with us and for lunch afterward. If you need a ride, let me know!"

Share. During this Easter season, we are urged in the Scriptures to be people who reveal the joy of the risen Lord and share him with others. As St. Pope John Paul II said, "We are the Easter people and hallelujah is our song." As you think about your family, friends, or parish community, is there someone in need of a little extra joy? Someone who has lost a loved one? Or a person struggling with ill health who could use a spark of joy? Consider spiritually "adopting" an Easter friend and find ways to let them know that you care—by making a meal, sending them notes, or taking them out for coffee or lunch.

Prepare. Coming fifty days after Easter, the feast of Pentecost comes from the Greek word *pentecost*, which means "fiftieth." The Scriptures point to the Holy Spirit coming in tongues of fire on this day, so wearing red to Mass is a subtle nod to this. Praying the prayer Come Holy Spirit as a family is especially apt on this day. Celebrate with fire-themed food (grill or hibachi) or a simple fruit salad because it is so very important to nurture the fruits of the Holy Spirit in our lives. The fruit of the Holy Spirit include love, joy, peace, patience, gentleness, kindness, and self-control.

There are so many ways to live our Catholic faith, and this appendix includes some easy ways to move more in tune with the liturgical year. Although not discussed here, Divine Mercy Sunday and Halloween, All Saints' Day, and All Souls' Day are also important times when families can uplift their faith in simple but meaningful ways. Remembering that faith is caught more than taught and living liturgically grounds our family in the sacred and precious traditions and rituals of our Catholic faith.

Take It Home

Key Takeaways

- The word *Advent* is derived from the Latin word *adventus*, which means "coming."
- A single candle in the window during Advent is a tradition that developed in Ireland but has since spread around the world.
- Advent and Christmas are two distinct seasons and should be acknowledged and celebrated as such.
- Lent is a time to consider the needs of others in prayer, fasting, and almsgiving.
- Holy Week is the most sacred week of the liturgical year for Christians.
- If you want your family to live liturgically, then mimic the rhythm of what is happening at church in your home.
- Within Easter the profound truth of our faith rests: Jesus Christ was crucified, died, and was buried and rose again on the third day.

Reflect and Journal

A conversation jar with several questions can also be a great way for family members to interweave faith into daily life. This is especially helpful if there are middle or high school children in the family. You can buy a pretty jar or paint a mason jar with whatever you want to call your "conversation starter" jar.

Discussion Topics

Questions	Reflections
Where did I see God today in my family, at school, in the community?	
What did I do today to be Christ to someone?	
How did Jesus speak to me today?	
How am I living liturgically at this time?	
Was there anything that happened to me that I would like to talk about?	
How can I make tomorrow better than today?	
What is God calling me to at this moment?	
What am I most thankful for in this present moment?	

Scripture quotes can be added as appropriate with some simple sharing around the table.

Practice: The Spiritual and Corporal Works of Mercy

The Catholic Church has a rich tradition of carrying out acts of service and charity. The spiritual and corporal works of mercy are actions that we carry out to alleviate the suffering of others. They are divided into two categories:

The corporal works of mercy: the focus is on material and physical needs.	The spiritual works of mercy: the focus is on emotional and spiritual needs.
Feed the hungry.	Instruct the ignorant.
Shelter the homeless.	Counsel the doubtful.
Clothe the naked.	Admonish the sinner.
Visit the sick and imprisoned.	Bear wrongs patiently.
Bury the dead.	Forgive offenses willingly.
Give alms to the poor.	Comfort the afflicted/burdened.

The corporal and spiritual works of mercy should permeate our entire lives, not be carried out only during Lent and forgotten about the rest of the year. Every month you could choose one of the works of mercy to focus on, research what it means, and practice carrying it out individually and together as a family.

Pray: Candle in the Window

On Christmas Eve, I would encourage you to take up this tradition of the candle in the window to remember those who are persecuted for their faith but also those who have abandoned the practice of faith. You can use a battery-operated candle to place in the window or simply light a candle as a symbol of this tradition elsewhere in your home.

May your home be a light to welcome and inspire others to grow in love and the practice of faith. As you light the candle, pray this simple prayer:

> May your Christmas be filled with the light of the Son,
> From whom comes our salvation, over darkness He's won.

> May the light of Jesus radiate from your heart
>   warm and pure,
> To family and friends and especially the poor.

> May the candle in your window
>   be a light at the inn
> of your hearth, heart, and home,
>   to stranger and kin.

> Amen.

Recommended Resources

For you: Gary Jansen's *Station to Station: An Ignatian Journey through the Stations of the Cross* provides a scriptural overview of the way of the cross to focus our hearts and minds on Jesus' anguish and death. Walking through each station, we see the unique ways in which Jesus responded to suffering, and we are challenged to react similarly in our own struggles.

For your children: The Shepherd's Story, by Jimmy Dunne, is a fresh perspective on the Christmas story. It provides readers with a profound experience alongside a courageous shepherd boy who is searching for meaning in life.

Conclusion: It's Our Time to Rise and Shine!

What a whirlwind journey we have been on! If your head is spinning with "all the things" that you could do to grow your family in faith, take a deep breath and remember that you've got this. Your children were given to you by God because God trusts you with them. As the old maxim goes, "Don't let the perfect be the enemy of the good," meaning don't strive for perfection, just be the best you can be and do the best you can do. Keeping your own peace while helping your children develop a sense of inner peace and resilience is possible even amid the whirlwind of family life. So, let's talk a little bit about peace.

Give Peace a Chance

We live in a fast-paced and increasingly anxiety-ridden world that is clearly affecting our social, emotional, physical, mental, and spiritual health, but especially the well-being of children. Studies published in the *Journal of Developmental and Behavioral Pediatrics* based on data collected from the National Survey of Children's Health indicate significantly increased rates of anxiety among children, youth, and young adults. Between ages 6 and 17, researchers found a 20 percent increase in diagnoses of anxiety between 2007 and 2012; the rate of depression over the same period ticked up 0.2 percent. These figures do not take into account the past few years of turmoil due to the effects of the COVID-19 pandemic and so are likely to be higher.

The phrase "deaths of despair" or "diseases of despair" comes from the groundbreaking work of the economists Anne Case and Sir Angus Deaton. Their 2015 paper "Rising Morbidity and Mortality in Midlife among White Non-Hispanic Americans in the 21st Century" reveals a startling increase in midlife mortality in white Americans. Since 2005, many leading causes of death, including stroke, cancer, heart disease, and lung disease, have all been decreasing. But deaths from drugs, alcohol, and suicide—what some call "deaths of despair"—have been steadily on the rise. "Deaths of despair" continue to affect every family today regardless of background, ethnicity, and economic reality.

Various research studies affirm that younger Americans are particularly affected. According to reports released by the public health groups Trust for America's Health and Well Being Trust, between 2007 and 2017, drug-related deaths increased by 108 percent among adults ages 18 to 34, alcohol-related deaths increased by 69 percent, and suicides increased by 35 percent. This report drew on Centers for Disease Control and Prevention data. Altogether, about 36,000 millennials died "deaths of despair" in 2017, with fatal drug overdoses being the biggest cause.

As people of faith, we know that mental, physical, and emotional health are interwoven with spiritual health. If we neglect the spiritual health conversation, we do so at our peril. It is clear that many people, our loved ones and even ourselves, have drowned or are continuing to drown in a world of despair filled with alcohol, drugs, and the absence of spirituality. If society continues to ignore the importance of spiritual health, it's likely that we will see deaths of despair continue to rise. If spirituality is a way for us to live out what we most value—our relationships with God and with others—it is the seam that keeps us all connected as humanity.

One of the issues many of our children face that can rob them of their peace is being teased about their faith. Choosing faith in a culture of FOMO (fear of missing out) or YOLO (you only live once) makes it a priority to cultivate a peaceful space to explore faith and belief. Providing a sanctuary for reflection, prayer, and thoughtful conversation in our homes can cultivate a deeper sense of peace for our families. Our homes can be "anchor spaces" that children come back to again and again no matter what challenges they face in life. Here are a few ideas to cultivate a more peaceful home.

Keep it simple. Nick from Kentucky reminds us: "You don't have to do 'all the things' and you don't have to be perfect. Do what works for you and your family. It's OK to just do the simple things. Go to Mass on Sunday. Say grace before meals. Pray with your family every night. Pick a few feast days and celebrate them. Try to say something good about Jesus every day. If you don't feel up to it, then start with what you do feel up to doing. Don't be too hard on yourself, and don't be too hard on your kids. Ask God to help you to be better for your children and He will. Love God. Love your neighbor. Love your kids."

Avoid too much "busyness." Consider your home and your schedules. While we want our children to be well-rounded human beings, often the pace of school and extracurricular activities leaves little downtime. Not every night needs to be filled with something. Limit activities if the balance between busyness and rest feels off-balance.

Family meals. Put a premium on eating together as a family for at least one meal a day, more if possible. If this isn't doable every day, set a goal for a minimum number of meals that you all can eat together. Many of the families I interviewed for this book indicated that mealtimes were precious times for everyone to connect with each other and that these small moments were the greatest building blocks of faith. "I've found that it's not the traditions that we do once a year that make the biggest impact or are remembered most. It's the daily things. Two specific examples are listening to Christian music on the radio in the car and praying before meals and at bedtime"—this is from Carrie and Paul, who travel between Wisconsin, California, and Hawaii with their six children.

A calm environment. Cast a critical eye on your home environment, particularly your child's bedroom space. While bright colors and clutter, particularly in bedrooms, is common, for children struggling with anxiety and depression this can be very difficult. Noise also comes through visual distractions such as loud colors or cluttered spaces, making it difficult to focus. Playing Christian music as a backdrop in the home can be helpful; so too can Gregorian chant be helpful in changing the mood in the house. Leave ample time for silence with no television, radio, or social media on occasion.

Contemplative prayer. Prayer is one of our tools to help us to stay connected to each other and more deeply to God. Introduce children to more contemplative prayer forms such as the *Suscipe* of St. Ignatius of Loyola, the Prayer of the Heart, or the Jesus Prayer.

Incorporate reflection. Start with one or two minutes and progress to ten minutes. A simple technique is as follows: Dim the lights slightly, asking everyone to close their eyes and to notice their breathing. Ask everyone to take three deep breaths in and three deep breaths out. As everyone continues to sit in silence, read a passage of Scripture or offer a simple prayer of the heart. Allow time for a few moments of silence and then ask everyone to open their eyes. You can incorporate a Scripture verse during this time such as "Do not worry about anything, but in everything by prayer and supplication with thanksgiving let your requests be made known to God. And the peace of

God, which surpasses all understanding, will guard your hearts and your minds in Christ Jesus" (Phil. 4:6–7).

It is my hope that all those who read this book will be inspired to parent their children and support their grandchildren in a way that glorifies God. As Catholics it is imperative that we raise our children to be joyful, thoughtful saints-in-training who transform the world for Jesus Christ. In a Facebook post dated February 12, 2022, Tim Glemkowski sums it up best:

> I don't want my kids to "stay Catholic."
> I want them to fall in love with God.
> I want them to experience the incredible adventure
>   He has for them.
> I want them to learn to love, without counting the cost.
> I want them to know the quiet intimacy of a daily Mass
>   and the abiding peace of a good Confession.
> I want them to be surrendered, trustful, free.
> I want them to be unshakably confident in who they are
>   because of what God has done.
> I want them to be inquisitive, well read, and wise.
> I want them to see God, everywhere and in everyone.
> I don't want my kids to "stay Catholic" . . .
>   I beg that God would make them great saints.

Amen! Children are not little problems to be solved but mysterious beings with their own thoughts, feelings, and behaviors. We can only do our best as parents and rely on God's help. The rest is up to them; as Anne Frank reminds us: "The final forming of a person's character lies in their own hands."

Rise and shine, just like Jesus, my friends, because it's great to be Catholic!

A Special Dedication

In memory of my dear friend, peacemaker
Bishop David G. O'Connell,
who passed into eternal life on February 18, 2023.
Bishop David loved Jesus, the Blessed Mother,
and every person he encountered. He taught me to pray
from the depth of my being with the Holy Spirit.
He will live forever in our hearts.

"You have gone no further from us
than to God, and God is very near."

—Irish expression

About the Author

Encourager, storyteller, author, and popular speaker, Julianne Stanz has ministered in the Diocese of Green Bay, Wisconsin, for more than twenty years. She is a consultant to the United States Conference of Catholic Bishops in the areas of youth, evangelization, and catechesis. By far, her favorite role in life is wife and mother to her three children. She is married to Wayne and they live by the shores of Lake Michigan, where she spends her time hunting for beach glass, gardening, and drinking tea.

Julianne strives to infuse her writings, talks, and retreats with snippets of spiritual wisdom sprinkled with a dose of Irish hospitality and humor. You can catch up with her at www.juliannestanz.com.